The Art of the Book

FROM MEDIEVAL MANUSCRIPT TO GRAPHIC NOVEL

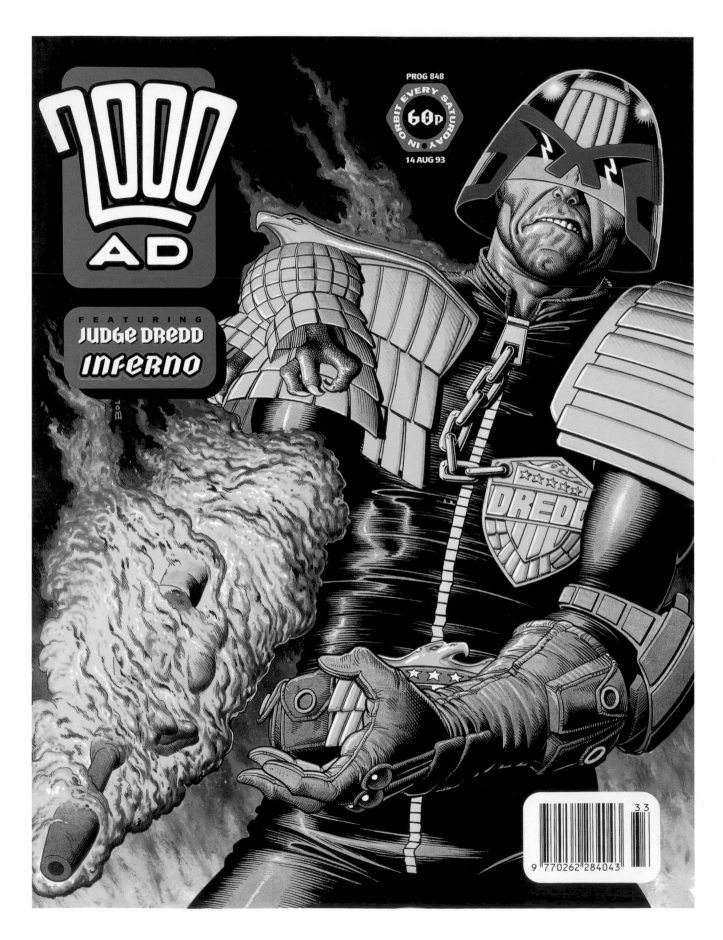

The Art of the Book

FROM MEDIEVAL MANUSCRIPT TO GRAPHIC NOVEL

EDITED BY JAMES BETTLEY

DISTRIBUTED IN NOR ... ARRY N. ABRAMS, INC.

First published by V&A Publications, 2001
V&A Publications
160 Brompton Road
London SW3 1HW

James Bettley asserts his moral right to be
identified as the author of this book.

Distributed in North America by
Harry N. Abrams, Incorporated, New York
ISBN: 0-8109-6572-0
(Harry N. Abrams, Inc.)

Designed by Cara Gallardo, Area

V&A photography by Richard Davis and
Dominic Naish

Printed in Hong Kong

Illustrations

Jacket Front: *Jazz* (see page 69)

Jacket Back: *Maus: a survivor's tale*
(see page 139) *Missal (Use of St Denis)* (see
page 16)

Frontispiece: *2000 AD*
(see page 143)

Harry N. Abrams, Inc.
100 Fifth Avenue
New York, N.Y. 10011
www.abramsbooks.com

Contents

ACKNOWLEDGEMENTS

A work of this nature is very much a collaborative project, and owes much to the input not just of the present contributors but of generations of staff and others who have catalogued the Library's collections and written about them. Some of their names can be found under FURTHER READING, as the authors of books, articles and catalogues that are constantly referred to by staff and users of the Library.

The individual chapters were compiled by James Bettley, Carlo Dumontet, Simon Ford, Anne Stevenson Hobbs, Elizabeth James, John Meriton, Eoin Shalloo and Jan van der Wateren, with additional contributions by Bernadette Archer, Katherine Coombs, Denise Drake, Jonathan Hopson, Leon Leigh, Richard Loveday, Patrick Perratt, Marc Ward and Eva White. Further help has been given by Malcolm Baker, Chiara Barontini, Guy Baxter, Elizabeth Bonython, Anthony Burton, Neil Crawford, Doug Dodds, Assunta Ferrera, Harry Gilonis, Françoise Lévèque, the late Ronald Horton, Serena Kelly, Liliane Lijn, Paul McQuail, Tomoko Masaki, Andrew Norris, David Pearson, Ian Rakoff, Andrew Russell, Justin G. Schiller, Rowan Watson and Michael Trevillian Wright.

INTRODUCTION

The National Art Library is one of the hidden treasures of the Victoria & Albert Museum. Its collections are large – over a million volumes, with a similar quantity of archive material – but they do not, on the whole, lend themselves to being displayed, and they are seen mostly by students and researchers, and only to a limited extent by the general public. Most visitors to the V&A probably go away without coming across the Library at all; if they do, they probably assume that it is for the use of Museum staff only. In fact, the NAL is freely available to all who wish to use it, and its physical location, on the south side of the Pirelli Garden, is symbolic of its place at the heart of Museum. Its history, its purpose and its collections are further indications of its central role in the life and activities of the V&A.

The NAL has three objectives. It is the Museum's library. It supports the work of the curators and provides background material relating to the objects on display; it is responsible for managing the Museum's administrative archive; and, given that no museum can collect everything in its field, it provides information about other examples of artefacts and works of art that complement the Museum's own collections. Secondly, it is a curatorial department in its own right. It collects books as objects and as works of art, to illustrate the history of the design of the book. Books may therefore be collected which, regardless of their subject matter, are or contain examples of fine binding, printing, and illustration, as well as the more recent genres

of *livres d'artistes* and book art. Thirdly, it is, simply, the National Art Library. It is the leading library in its subject area in the country, and as such, is the library to which all serious researchers in the many subjects that constitute 'art' in its broadest sense resort.

In fact, it started out as none of these things. The NAL, like the V&A itself, owes its origin to concerns, in the 1830s, that Britain was lagging behind its European rivals in the design of its industrial products. In 1835 the House of Commons appointed a Select Committee on Arts and Manufactures, as a result of which the Schools of Design were established in Somerset House in 1837 in premises provided by the Royal Academy. The Schools were administered by the Board of Trade, and their purpose was to train craftsmen in the rudiments of design. The Schools were empowered to purchase plaster casts and books, and in retrospect, these can be seen to have been the origins of the Museum and the Library respectively. The Library was small, and overwhelmingly practical; in 1846, the 850 volumes were described as:

> treatises on the history, theoretic principles and practice of Fine Art in general, elementary manuals on Architecture, Practical Geometry, Optics, Perspective, Anatomy, and every obtainable work on the application of art to manufactures and decoration.

The Schools of Design experienced difficulties, and in 1852 were placed in the charge of Henry Cole, a civil servant who had already proved himself by reforming the Public Record Office, and had just played an important part in organising the Great Exhibition of 1851. Responsibility for the Schools was transferred to the new Department of Practical Art and they moved to Marlborough House; at the same time the first full-time librarian was appointed, an art historian called Ralph Wornum who went on to be the Keeper of the National Gallery. It was Wornum who first gave the Library a more academic character, buying books of a consciously art-historical nature; he also opened the Library to the general public, and started a classified catalogue. The catalogue which he published in 1855 – when the number of books in the Library stood at about 5,000 volumes, as well as 100 portfolios and prints and drawings – explained the classification, which was based upon the system used to classify the arts and trades at the Great Exhibition. Wornum was able to say that the Library contained 'a range of subjects directly bearing upon upwards of two hundred trades now carried on in the metropolis' which, 'to avoid anything like vagueness', he went on to list. In spite of his own leanings, therefore, the emphasis of the Library was still firmly practical; but it is interesting to see the importance which was attached, then as now, to providing the sort of background material that is indispensable in the study, as well as the practice, of art: anatomy and physiology, geometry and perspective, heraldry, seals and crests, natural history in its application to art (botany, conchology, entomology, mineralogy and zoology), and topography and guides all have their place in Wornum's scheme. This breadth of approach has resulted in a library whose holdings are rich in all sorts of unexpected areas, of which it is never safe to say, without first checking the catalogue, that it would not contain a particular book.

In 1857 Cole took the Schools and its Library to South Kensington, to a site purchased out of the profits of the Great Exhibition, and so the South Kensington Museum – renamed the Victoria & Albert Museum in 1899 – was born. Although housed in rooms that were far from suitable, these were years of great expansion for the Library, when it acquired some of its greatest treasures. Wornum's successor was J.C. Robinson, who did more than anyone to build up the collections of the Museum as a whole during those early years, and he in turn was succeeded in 1868 by R.H. Soden Smith. Soden Smith remained in office until his death in 1890 and during that time expanded the Library twelvefold, taking it to over 60,000 volumes. He was himself an eminent collector of books and it was he who was responsible for a number of the Library's distinguished acquisitions of specimens of the art of the book: illumination, binding, typography and illustration. Moreover, it was during his tenure that the Library received three of its greatest bequests, in 1868, 1869, and 1876: the collection of illustrated books formed by the Revd Chauncy Hare Townshend, which included a set of Audubon's *Birds of America*; the working library of the Revd Alexander Dyce, which included a collection of Restoration plays; and, greatest of all, the library of John Forster, critic, journalist and historian, and the friend, biographer and literary executor of Charles Dickens. This last bequest brought some of the Library's greatest treasures, including manuscripts, corrected proofs and first editions of Dickens's novels, and three notebooks of Leonardo da Vinci (see pp. 43, 78 and 85). The Library also received valuable books as part of the major bequest to the Museum by John Jones in 1882, and in 1880 purchased the Piot Collection of works relating to pageants, fêtes and ceremonies.

Such expansion necessitated improvements in both the catalogue and the accommodation of the Library. The latter was achieved – up to a point – in 1884, when purpose-built premises for the Library on the south side of the quadrangle were completed. Construction had proceeded slowly; the new building had been approved in 1876, and started in May 1878, and although the Reading Room was ready to be furnished in 1881 the interior was not finally ready until 1884. The new Library provided accommodation for about 80 readers and consisted of a suite of three rooms. The Reading Room was much as it still is, fitted with desks and book-cases; the Centre Room was used for consulting large items, including prints and drawings; while the West Room was used to store and display prints and was, unlike today, accessible to the public.

Unfortunately the book stacks that were an integral part of the scheme were never built, and by 1890 the shelves in the Reading Rooms were already full. The Library was the first part of the Museum designed from the outset to be lit by electricity rather than gas, which was recognised to be particularly harmful to books because of the fumes which it gave off. The mahogany fittings were designed by John Taylor, architect to the Office of Works, with mosaic panels on the exterior and plaster overdoors on the interior by Reuben Townroe.

Although clearly not straightforward, the question of accommodation seems to have been dealt with more easily than that of the catalogue. In 1863 Cole had appointed the architect John Hungerford Pollen as the Museum's General Superintendent of Catalogues, and between them they devised a plan for cataloguing the Library which displays the sort of lateral thinking which sometimes only an outsider can bring to a task. Given that the Library was expanding at such a rate,

the task of publishing a catalogue was futile, because it would go out of date so quickly. The answer, therefore, was to compile a complete catalogue of all the books on art that had ever been published, and to indicate which were in the Library. The flaw in this logic, of course, is that new books were being published, and therefore the *Universal Catalogue of Books on Art*, as it was called, would itself go out of date; but either this did not occur to Cole and Pollen, or they thought it irrelevant, and the catalogue was published in book form in 1870. The *Universal Catalogue* defined the scope of the Library and it was in recognition of this that it was then renamed the National Art Library.

The *Universal Catalogue* is still useful but it has always been confusing, leading readers to think that books are held by the Library when this is not the case, and what neither Cole nor Pollen seem to have understood was that the answer to catalogues going out of date was simply not to publish them in any conventional sense. Before his death in 1890 Soden Smith embarked upon an overhaul of the catalogue, combining the *Universal Catalogue* with the various supplements that had been published since in a series of guard-books, some of which are still in use; but it was his successor, W.H. James Weale, who introduced the card catalogue which remained in use until the computerisation of the Library in 1987. The microfiche of this catalogue is still an essential tool for anyone using the Library. Weale's other great achievement in this area was to establish cataloguing rules, based on those of the British Museum, and to train his staff rigorously.

Weale was not an easy character, and his forthright denunciation of the management of the Museum to a Select Committee of the House of Commons in 1897 led to his sudden departure from the V&A in that year. His legacy included not just the catalogue (his successor, G.H. Palmer, whom he had trained, devised the subject index which complements the card catalogue), but also some its most notable medieval manuscripts. This was one of Weale's particular areas of expertise, and he purchased the fourteenth-century missal of Saint-Denis in 1891 and the fifteenth-century manuscript of Pliny's *Historia naturalis* in 1896 (see pp. 16 and 19).

The change of name to the Victoria & Albert Museum in 1899 marked the occasion of the laying of the foundation stone of the new block, designed by Aston Webb, that now forms the frontage to Cromwell Road. The completion of this work – the new building was opened by King Edward VII in 1909 – was accompanied by a complete reorganisation of the Museum, involving the creation of the departmental structure that is still broadly in place today. This had a number of consequences for the Library, perhaps the greatest of which was the removal of the collection of prints and drawings to the new Department of Engraving, Illustration and Design (since combined with the Department of Painting to form the Department of Prints, Drawings and Paintings). This made space available in the Centre Room for the shelving of books, additional storage being provided in the area to the west of the quadrangle.

One result of the increased exhibition space in the Museum was that the Library was given its own 'Gallery for the Art of the Book', in which to display 'the best examples of lettering, writing, illumination, types, type-ornaments … and book bindings'. This gallery, which remained in use until the creation of the Twentieth-Century Gallery in 1978, was located to the west of the Library, and there was thus the opportunity, now lost, to enter the Museum from Exhibition Road, proceed through the Gallery of the Art of the Book and enter the Library through the West Room, to the Centre Room where the catalogues were housed, and finally reach the calm of the Reading Room. Now that the West Room is restricted to staff, and is completely occupied with storage and offices, the entrance to the Library is via the Reading Room, resulting in more traffic past the desks than is ideal. Aston Webb's vision was for a grand staircase coming up into the Centre Room from the hall below, but that was never achieved. The loss of the gallery was a great blow to the Library, but some presence is achieved in the Museum through a series of temporary displays outside the Library and elsewhere, and books are included as examples of design in a number of galleries throughout the Museum. Loans are also made to internal and external exhibitions.

The next fifty years were ones of quiet consolidation rather than dramatic innovation, a change of pace reflected by the adoption of 'Victoria & Albert Museum Library' as the generally accepted name ('National Art Library' was revived in the 1970s). The change was significant. The Library ceased to be so outward-looking and all-embracing. The emphasis was on serving the needs of the Museum's curators and a select group of scholars, rather than students or the world at large, and certainly not the artisans for whom the Library was originally established.

This is not to say that the Library did not continue to develop. Its collections grew, and it became firmly established as a major academic library serving an international readership of art historians and researchers. The Library was in the forefront of collecting *livres d'artistes* and also, under the influence of a Deputy Keeper, James Wardrop, calligraphy. Children's books, which had always been collected as examples of illustration, assumed a more important place in the Library with the bequest in 1961 by Guy Little of his collection of children's books, bindings and illustrated books (see pp. 103 and 107). This was followed in 1973 by the Linder Bequest of material on Beatrix Potter (see p. 108). Less expected is the Hutton Bequest of 1911, of works on swordsmanship, self-defence, weapons, arms and armour. The Harrod Collection of illustrated and trade-bound books was acquired in 1933 (see p. 52); the Clements Collection of heraldic bindings in 1940 (see p. 60); the Larianov Collection of material relating to the visual and performing arts in 1961.

By 1951 the collection numbered some 300,000 volumes, and books were being acquired at the rate of about 5,000 a year. Further space was desperately needed, and this was achieved in 1966–7 by the drastic expedient of inserting three floors of book stacks into Aston Webb's Central Court. This had the desired effect of creating additional storage, and at the time was justified as it brought to an end 'the visual conflict between the character of the museum exhibits – early medieval art – and the Victorian [sic] renaissance detail of the original room design', but fashions change and the removal of the stacks, to open up this great space once again, has been talked about in recent years as part of a general programme to restore the Museum's interiors to their original appearance.

Such a reversal would only be possible if alternative space were found elsewhere. Further storage has since been provided on the ground floor and, most recently, in the Crypt, but more ambitious schemes – including excavating beneath the Pirelli Garden, taking over the Henry Cole Wing, and relocating to the former Public Record Office in Chancery Lane – have all come to nothing. Photographs eventually followed prints and drawings in 1977, thus freeing up a little more space within the Library.

By this time, the Library was facing a crisis of a different order. In the late 1960s and early '70s there was a dramatic rise in interest in Art History as an academic discipline; the new polytechnics offered degree courses in design, design history, graphics and fashion, and television encouraged a general interest in the visual arts. This was accompanied by a huge increase in the number of books being published on the arts. The demands placed upon the Library were unprecedented, and it was unable to cope: it did not have sufficient staff, nor sufficient funds, and it was not geared up to meet the needs of a new generation of library users. The appointment of Elizabeth Esteve-Coll, a professional librarian with a background in academic libraries, transformed the Library, and the extent of her achievement was recognised by her appointment as Director of the Museum in 1988. She was succeeded as Chief Librarian by Jan van der Wateren, who retired in 2000. Perhaps the most significant development of this last period has been the computerisation of the Library's catalogues, culminating in a programme to convert all the existing card catalogues to electronic format, which will be completed by the end of 2003. Once that has been achieved, it will be possible to say, with a degree of accuracy that has not been possible for many years, exactly how many books the Library contains.

As it is, one can only indicate the scope of the Library's collection in broad terms. Much has been said already about what is to be found in the NAL. A number of the special, closed collections have been mentioned, and there have been other recent acquisitions of this sort which have built on existing strengths but also taken the Library in new directions: the Osman-Gidal Collection, for example, of mostly European magazines, and which was formed to document the use of photoreportage, was acquired in 1990–91, and the Rakoff Collection of comics and graphics novels in 1990 (see pp. 131, 132 and 139). The creation of the Archive of Art and Design in 1978 (see p. 77) has led to the acquisition of substantial archives of firms and individuals.

As well as taking in other people's collections, the Library has also been developing its own special collections. These include collections of fine bindings and noteworthy trade bindings; illustrated books; writing and lettering books; fine typography; examples of modern book and magazine design; livres d'artistes, artists' books and, most recently, book art. There are extensive collections of official and popular publications relating to the Great Exhibition, and a collection of the V&A's own publications since its inception, of which a bibliography (together with a chronology of the V&A's exhibitions) was published in 1998. The Library also collects ephemeral items, and has rich collections of commercial typography ('jobbing printing'), dating mainly from the 1930s, and of trade catalogues. The Library actively collects current trade literature, in consultation with relevant Museum departments, and also has a programme to acquire exhibition catalogues from smaller galleries that might otherwise go unrecorded. Since 1996, the NAL has also received from the British Library copies of smaller exhibition catalogues deposited with them. The NAL's holdings of auction sale catalogues are particularly strong, including runs of priced catalogues, and date back to 1678. The Library's collections of manuscripts, both illuminated and documentary, are described in Chapters 1 and 4.

All these individual collections combine to create a resource which is unequalled in the field, and which people travel across the world to use. Yet they are additional to the Library's principal activity, which is the acquisition and cataloguing of newly published books and peri-

odicals on art. The subject areas in which the Library collects have been refined over the years, a reflection partly of the changing emphasis of the Library from practical to academic, partly of the strengths of other libraries with which it would be futile and wasteful to compete; but the underlying aim is still to interpret art in its broadest sense and to provide works which place artistic activity in its social, economic and political context. A detailed Policy for the Development of the Collections was published in 1993, describing the collections, the subject areas in which material is collected, and to what level, ranging from minimal to comprehensive. Holdings are particularly strong in the areas covered by the Museum itself, and the Library follows the same geographical boundaries as the Museum, confining itself largely to the major artistic traditions of Europe, Asia and North Africa, collecting in other areas (Oceania, sub-Saharan Africa and the Americas) only insofar as they relate to, or throw light upon, the European tradition. These limits were set in the middle of the nineteenth century; they are becoming increasingly difficult to maintain, as society becomes more international and the differences between 'natives' and 'settlers' disappear, and will no doubt disappear themselves before very long.

The Library currently acquires about 18,000 items a year, of which about two-thirds are monographs and the remainder are serial parts. Of the monographs, less than half are purchases, the rest consisting of gifts and exchanges, sales catalogues, trade literature, and exhibition catalogues.

With the exception of the final chapter, the works described in this book are mostly selected from the Library's Special Collections, and are exceptional, if not unique. Inevitably, further acquisitions in these areas are relatively rare, because they tend to be expensive, and the funds available for purchase are required to keep up-to-date with new publications; much depends upon the generosity of donors, in the form of gifts or bequests. It is still possible to build up some collections of potential future value at little cost – comics is one such area, which has been actively developed in recent years – but acquisitions of illuminated manuscripts or fine bindings are few and far between. Conservation and cataloguing are priorities in these and other areas, rather than acquisition, which at least makes it easier to achieve the most important aim of all, which is to make the Library's collections accessible to as wide an audience as possible. Thanks to the automated catalogue, freely available on the World Wide Web, more and more people know what is in the Library, even if they still have to come to South Kensington to look at what they find; and the principal justification for maintaining a library such as the National Art Library is that it should be used.

In selecting the objects for this book, we have tried to reflect the breadth of the Library's holdings, as well as its strengths. Much of what is important in the Library has had to be left out: there are no trade catalogues represented here, for example, nor auction catalogues. A selection such as this cannot really convey the range of the Library's holdings of periodicals: just under 11,000 titles, of which about 2,300 are current. But what it *can* do is to touch on major aspects of book production, and the documentation of art and design, ranging from an illuminated manuscript of 1350 to the private view-card of an avant-garde exhibition of 1998: 650 years of what is generally taken to be progress.

Chapter 1 is devoted to the most conspicu-ously artistic aspect of book production: the use of illumination and calligraphy to decorate pages of text. Chapter 2 looks at a development of this, the use of illustrations in printed books, specifically those produced during the nineteenth century when there were huge changes in the development of printing techniques. The reproduction of images is one of the points where art meets craft and industry, and the same can be said for bindings (Chapter 3), which range from the purely practical to the highly artistic to the purely commercial, but all requiring considerable skill in design and execution. Chapter 4 looks at documentary manuscripts, the often mundane material which is valued for its content rather than its appearance, and which is a means to an end rather than an end in itself, although some such documents may acquire an aesthetic value in the eyes of later generations. Chapters 5 and 6 look at two types of material represented in the Library – children's books and comics – which extend the scope of this book beyond work that is primarily concerned with fine art or craft but nonetheless require great flair and expertise in terms of art and design. Two further genres, self-consciously artistic, are then explored: the use of typography to create images out of text on the page (Chapter 7), and book art (Chapter 8), 'where the book is a work of art in itself'. Finally, in Chapter 9, a selection of works published in the 1990s looks at the way in which the relationship between contemporary art and publishing not only produces important and striking publications, but also contributes to the success of the art it is documenting: tomorrow's art history in the making.

1 Illumination (the Decorated Page)

'The Decorated Page' was the title of an exhibition held at the V&A in 1971; it was devoted principally to illuminated manuscripts and books but included also some items of twentieth-century calligraphy. The scope of this section is similar, because what these items have in common is that words are recorded on a page in a way that results in a work of art. What changes in the course of the 600 years represented by the objects included here is the reason for that decoration.

In 1350, the approximate date of the missal from Saint-Denis, all books were copied out by hand. By this time book production was no longer exclusively monastic, and larger towns had lay workshops employing scribes and illuminators, but the fact remains that a high proportion of the best, the most elaborate, and therefore the most expensive works were devotional in nature; and because they have been treasured ever since they were made these are the works which have tended to survive. The purpose of illumination was literally to light up the page, to make the text easier to read and more comprehensible by illustrating the subject matter, by breaking up blocks of text, and by giving a structure to the page. There was another very important aspect to the decoration, and that was to create a special work that was appropriate to a sacred subject, just as vestments or altar pieces were decorated as richly as funds allowed.

This remained broadly the case until the invention of printing. The principal purpose of manuscripts was to provide a text for conveying information or, in the case of a missal, instructions; further elaboration served a purpose that was partly practical, and partly symbolic, and in many cases was simply the result of the natural tendency of the scribe to embellish the page. With the advent of printing, however, the need to write out books by hand immediately disappeared; illumination and calligraphy became a much more deliberate and self-conscious activity, reserved for only the most special occasions. The art survived in the production of deeds and documents such as the Letters Patent of 1524, which in this case has the added interest of including a portrait miniature of the monarch, King Henry VIII, and shows the development of the miniature from being the embellishment of a manuscript to an art form in its own right. Deeds not unlike this, such as grants of arms, are still produced to this day, heraldry being particularly suited to the art of illumination.

Even more self-conscious was the revival of the art of illumination in the middle of the nineteenth century, soon followed by the virtual invention of calligraphy as an art form. The interest in both art forms was closely linked to the Gothic Revival in architecture and design generally, and was an inevitable consequence of the interest in all things medieval. Original medieval work was collected, and it was also copied by artists like Henry Shaw or published in facsimile, which in turn inspired a new generation of artists to create original work in the medieval style – a process aided by the invention of chromolithography, used by Owen Jones and Noel Humphreys to publish their influential works. The results were splendid but, unlike their medieval counterparts, intended to be admired rather than actually used. Illuminating, partly because of its often sacred character, became a respectable hobby for ladies, one that could be enjoyed even on Sundays. The period also saw an extraordinary fashion for illuminated addresses to mark anniversaries and other special events: Queen Victoria received over 2,000 such addresses for her Jubilee in 1887, and even more in 1897.

It was William Morris who, in characteristic manner, took up calligraphy and went back to first principles in order to learn for himself a technique that was all but obsolete. From him there descended a school of calligraphers – Edward Johnston, Eric Gill, Graily Hewitt, Heather Child – whose influence is still very much alive today and responsible for creating works which have a beauty and importance that may be far greater than the value of the information conveyed. The foundation of the Society of Scribes and Illuminators in 1921 indicated the coming of age of the revived art form.

The National Art Library has collected illuminated manuscripts since its foundation, for purposes which have changed over the years. Initially, examples of illumination were collected as part of the Museum's mission to make artefacts available to designers and workmen; the first were acquired in 1855, and were circulated to art schools outside London.

Ready-made collections were purchased, such as portfolios of cuttings and single leaves (cutting up medieval manuscripts was then a respectable activity, indulged by John Ruskin among others), and then complete illuminated manuscripts. Some works were acquired as much for their subject matter as their form: Cipriano Piccolpasso's *Tre libri dell'arte del vasaio*, for example, a manual on the potter's art, and Pliny's *Historia naturalis*, were acquired in 1869 and 1896 respectively. The collection was greatly enlarged in 1902–3 by George Reid of Dunfermline, whose bequest of 83 illuminated manuscripts was made with the particular intention that they be made available to students of lettering and illumination. Although most of these manuscripts are not of the highest quality, more modest and, in particular, incomplete examples, may be better for educational purposes than exceptional works. Other benefactors have included George Salting, David M. Currie and Sir Sydney Cockerell, the last a highly influential figure, through his encouragement and patronage, in the development of calligraphy in the twentieth century. It is in the latter area that acquisitions have mostly been made in recent years, largely as a result of the high price of medieval manuscripts, although exceptional works are still acquired, such as the *Two Trials of Joan of Arc*, when the opportunity arises.

Dagobert, the Stag, and St Denis

This missal was produced in Paris in 1350 for the royal abbey of Saint-Denis, which now lies in the northern suburbs of that city. The missal contains the liturgy for the mass, so was essential to the work of every priest: but only the most important clergy would own a manuscript of this quality. The close relationship that existed between the monarchy and Saint-Denis (which was the chief burial place for French kings) suggests that it may have been a royal donation to the abbey. The decoration consists of nearly 30 miniatures illustrating stories from the Bible and the lives of the saints, as well as decorative borders filled with realistic birds, butterflies and other creatures. Although the name of the illuminator is not known, his work has been identified in other manuscripts of the period, and he is seen to be influential in the development of a new naturalistic style of painting, introducing a treatment of space not seen before in French art. This interest in perspective was introduced to France by the illuminator Jean Pucelle in the first quarter of the fourteenth century, possibly following travels in Italy.

The page shown is one of two in the manuscript illustrating scenes from the legend of the founding of the abbey. The text is for the Office of the Relics of St Denis, and the scene within the initial at the top of the page shows the stag which, pursued by the future King Dagobert, took refuge in the church containing the remains of St Denis. A mysterious force prevented the hounds from entering. Although the perspective is crude in comparison with art of the Renaissance, there is a very clear impression of depth. The miniature overflows the frame of the initial 'O', the landscape receding into the distance and the architecture jutting out in front of the letter. Even the hounds playfully jump through the 'O' as though it were integral to the scene.

At the bottom of the page, two scenes in *grisaille* (i.e. painted largely in shades of grey) show St Denis appearing to Dagobert in a dream, and Dagobert being reconciled with his father, King Clothaire. Dagobert in these scenes is dressed in royal blue, with gold fleurs-de-lis.

MISSAL (USE OF ST DENIS)

Paris, *c.*1350. Parchment. 439 ff. 233 x 164 mm. Textura script in Latin. Accession no.: MSL/1891/1346 Pressmark: KRP.F.5

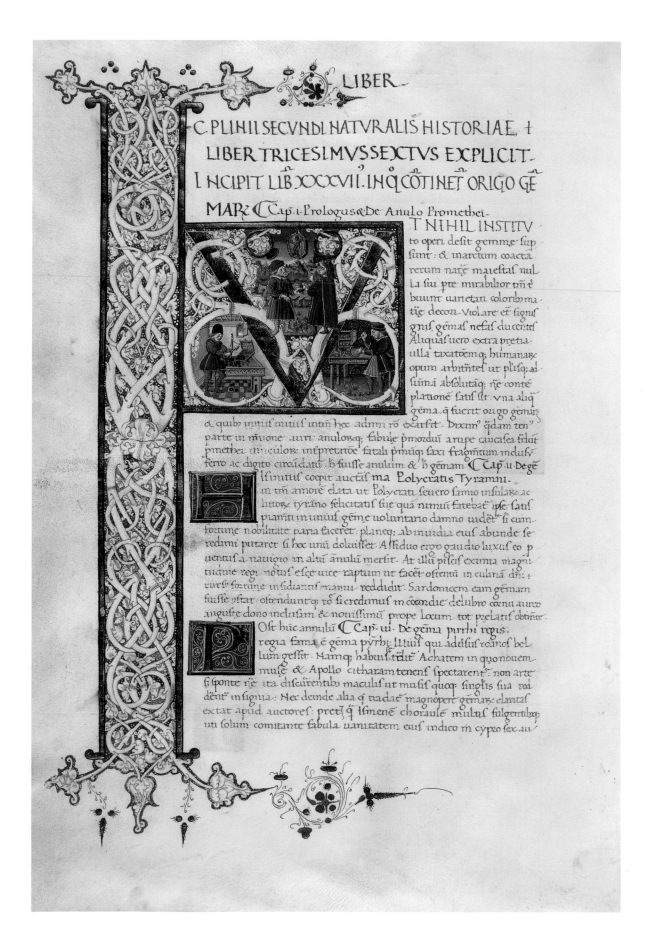

Historia naturalis

PLINY THE ELDER
(AD 23–79)
*NATURALIS
HISTORIAE LIBER
[PRIMUS]
TRICESIMUS
SEPTIMUS ET
ULTIMUS*

Rome, *c.*1465.
Parchment. 525 ff.
416 x 292 mm.
Humanistic script
in Latin.
Accession no.:
MSL/1896/1504
Pressmark: KRP.D.12

This lavish manuscript from Renaissance Italy is a copy of the *Historia naturalis* (Natural History) of Pliny the Elder, originally composed around AD 70. It was probably produced for Gregorio Lolli Piccolomini, a relation of Pope Pius II and an employee in his papal curia, whose arms appear amidst the decoration of the manuscript.

The Renaissance was a time of renewed interest in classical literature and culture. There was increasing book ownership amongst the upper classes of society, and classical texts had a central place in private libraries. The *Historia naturalis*, a vast compendium of facts, observations and myths about the natural and human worlds, had been valued throughout the Middle Ages as the chief authority on science. Later, interest focused on the chapters dealing with the arts: humanist authors such as Petrarch and Boccaccio are known to have read the text. It is still of much interest today as the only surviving contemporary account of art in the ancient world.

It was not only the choice of text that was influenced by Renaissance ideals. The appearance of the manuscripts, too, looked back to earlier styles. Whether it was actually believed that the models for the new styles were authentically ancient is uncertain. In fact, the white vine-stem decoration and Humanist script characteristically used for classical texts were based on north Italian manuscripts of the twelfth century. Humanist script replaced Gothic for all but liturgical manuscripts and its adoption by printers ensured its survival until the present day as the basis of roman typefaces.

Each of the 37 books of the Natural History begins with a decorated initial. Three of these are purely ornamental, but the rest contain scenes of contemporary life illustrating the following book. These illustrations have been attributed, although not without controversy, to the Florentine painter Giuliano Amedei. In the page shown, the 35th book (on painting) is introduced by three scenes of artisans at work: an artist painting a vaulted ceiling, an apprentice grinding pigments, and an artist working on *cassoni* (marriage chests). On the wall of the latter's studio are shields bearing the arms of Lolli and Piccolomini, a tribute to the manuscript's first owner.

Book of Hours of Margaret de Foix

This Book of Hours was produced in France in the 1470s, possibly for Margaret de Foix, the second wife of Francis II, Duke of Brittany. Although essentially a mass-produced item, it has been customised in a number of ways to suit the particular needs of its aristocratic owners.

The text itself gives no sign of having been written for a specific person. The liturgy follows the Use of Paris, which was widely employed in France at this time, and the saints listed in the calendar give no sign of localised usage. However, bound at the end of the manuscript is a prayer asking for an end to the sterility of Margaret. That this part of the manuscript is written in a different hand suggests that the main text was the standard production of a workshop.

Most of the decoration follows established patterns that would be expected from a book produced in a workshop of the period. Three distinct styles of border, representing the work of three different artists, are present in different parts of the manuscript. In the first style, twirling acanthus leaves are mixed with realistic flowers and fruit, and in the second style, the foliage is populated with birds and animals. The third style, towards the end of the manuscript, has a simpler foliage pattern on a ground of brushed gold, sometimes with animals and monsters.

Space would often be left in a manuscript for the inclusion of the owner's coat-of-arms, and this manuscript is no exception. Traces of a coat-of-arms, now largely erased, appear in three places. They seem to have shown the ducal arms of Brittany impaling the Foix arms.

The smaller miniatures follow conventional patterns, but a cycle of 12 full-page miniatures are of more interest. They are in an accomplished style that shows the influence of the fifteenth-century French master Jean Fouquet. Accompanying the office of Tierce, instead of the usual Annunciation to the Shepherds, there are scenes from Christ's Passion. This divergence from custom may well reflect the personal wishes of the owner. Particularly striking is the miniature introducing the Hours of the Cross, in which the Way of the Cross and the Crucifixion are combined into a single scene.

BOOK OF HOURS (USE OF PARIS)

France, c.1470s.
Parchment. 228 ff.
180 x 125 mm.
Bastarda script in Latin.
Accession no.:
L.2385-1910
(Salting no. 1222)
Pressmark: KRP.A.29

The Playfair Hours

BOOK OF HOURS (USE OF SARUM)

Rouen, *c.*1480s.
Parchment. 203 ff.
175 x 115 mm.
Bastarda script in Latin.
Accession no.:
MSL/1918/475
Pressmark: KRP.A.26

This manuscript was produced in a workshop in Rouen in the 1480s for a Scottish owner, possibly for the export market; it is generally known by the name of its owners in the nineteenth century, the Playfair family. The Book of Hours contains a set of texts for the private devotions of the laity, and at this period many moderately wealthy families would have possessed a copy, making it a suitable subject for mass-production.

The manuscript is lavishly illustrated, with 19 pages entirely filled with miniatures and decoration, and a further 41 smaller miniatures, each page being surrounded by a decorative border. The styles of the decoration are, however, heterogeneous. The work of seven different illuminators, as well as several scribes, has been identified. Their work would have been co-ordinated by a bookseller (or *libraire*), possibly for a particular customer. At the front of the manuscript, as with all Books of Hours, is the calendar, showing saints' days and feasts. This section appears to be a single unit of production, marked by a slightly different script and decorative style to any of those found elsewhere in the manuscript. Each month covers two pages, with a miniature covering nearly half a page. As was traditional for the calendar, the miniatures represent the labours of the months. The same, or similar, calendar illustrations have been identified in other Books of Hours from Rouen, showing that different artists, perhaps working in the same workshop, were using the same patterns. The illustration for May shows a gentleman and his lady hawking.

The text of the manuscript suggests it was intended for a Scottish owner. The form of the liturgy is the Use of Sarum, in use throughout the British Isles, and the calendar contains the names of some Scottish saints, little known elsewhere. However, although it came to the V&A from a Scottish owner, it does not seem to have arrived in Scotland until relatively late in its life. It could be that the original owner was from Scotland, but living in France; or that, rather than being produced to order, the manuscript was produced by a workshop for general stock.

The Two Trials of Joan of Arc

Joan of Arc was tried twice. The first trial, in 1431, resulted in her being burnt at the stake; the second resulted in her rehabilitation by the Church in 1456 after a seven-year retrial. This manuscript was commissioned by Diane of Poitiers, mistress of Henri II of France, in about 1538, and is one of the earliest sources both for the history of Joan herself and for the development of her cult. It is written in French, in a Gothic script, and as well as numerous decorated initials and borders there are five miniatures by the Master of Ango Hours. This important artist, who is known to have been working in Rouen in the 1520s, played a major role in introducing Italian design into France. The miniatures show scenes from the trials, including the only known early representation of Joan's mother; the page reproduced here is dominated by the seated figure of King Henry VI, and the central figure of the three in the foreground is thought to be Joan herself.

By 1569, the manuscript had come into the possession of Cardinal Jacques d'Armagnac (for which reason it is often referred to as the 'Armagnac' Manuscript), and it then passed, via his illegitimate daughter Fleurette, to the Villemeur family, whose births and deaths down to 1698 have been recorded at the beginning of the volume, in the manner of a family Bible. By the end of the eighteenth century, when it was acquired by Frederick North, 5th Earl of Guilford, there was renewed interest in Joan as a champion of the common people: Robert Southey's *Joan of Arc, an Epic Poem* appeared in 1796, and was a rebuttal of Voltaire's rationalist account of her as a religious extremist.

As well as being a beautiful piece of work in its own right, of high artistic and calligraphic merit, the manuscript therefore has great historical significance, throwing light upon the history of the cult of Joan, not just in the sixteenth century but also in the eighteenth – a process which led eventually to her canonisation in 1920. The manuscript was on loan to the Museum from 1959 until the death of its owner in 1991, but it returned to the NAL in 1998 after being accepted by HM Government in lieu of Inheritance Tax and allocated to the V&A.

[THE TWO TRIALS OF JOAN OF ARC]

French, commissioned *c.*1538 for Diane de Poitiers (the 'Armagnac' Manuscript).
Parchment. 86 ff.
280 x 188 mm.
Gothic script in French.
Accession no.: MSL/1998/3
Pressmark: Safe 2

King Henry VIII in Miniature

*LETTERS PATENT
WITH MINIATURE
OF HENRY VIII*

1524.
Parchment. 1 leaf.
Accession no.:
MSL/1999/6

'Letters patent' is the term used to describe a document issued by the monarch to confer some right, privilege, title, property or office – in this case, King Henry VIII was granting various properties in the parish of St Michael in Cornhill, London, to Thomas Forster. Such documents, being of great importance, were most elaborate, with decorative borders, and often, as in this case, a portrait miniature of the monarch. This particular letters patent, which dates from 1524, is a fine example of English Renaissance ornamentation; but its main importance lies in the portrait miniature of King Henry VIII.

The image is a bearded version of the separate portrait miniature of Henry VIII attributed to Lucas Hornebolte held by the Fitzwilliam Museum, Cambridge. This is generally accepted as the first known separate portrait miniature in England, which can be dated to between 1524 and 1526. It is the key image in any discussion of the development of the portrait miniature at the Court of Henry VIII and the role of Flemish illuminators in this development.

How exactly the letters patent image fits into the chronology of this development is not absolutely clear, because the image might have been added after the issue of the letters in 1524; but it is without doubt an important fragment of information, and illustrates beautifully the way that illumination – the practice of working on vellum in watercolour – was the root of miniature painting. The term 'miniature' does not in fact describe the size of these paintings, but the medium. Miniature

portraits developed from the art of painting manuscripts, and this type of painting was called 'limning'. Limning, and the more modern term 'illumination', derive from the Latin *luminare*, meaning to give light. 'Miniature', which caught on a hundred years after this document, was the Italian for illumination, *miniatura*, and comes from the Latin *minium* meaning red lead. It is only by association with Latin words such as *minor* that miniature has come to mean a small-scale version of anything.

The *Victoria Psalter*

The *Victoria Psalter* is the unofficial title of an illuminated edition of the Psalms of David that was published in parts in 1861–2 and dedicated to Queen Victoria. It has been said that Owen Jones considered it his masterpiece, and while it has proved to be of less enduring influence than his *The Grammar of Ornament* (see p. 51), it is nonetheless a remarkable *tour de force*.

Owen Jones had made a careful study of medieval illuminated manuscripts, and in 1844 collaborated with Henry Noel Humphreys on *The Illuminated Books of the Middle Ages*. But Jones was first and foremost a designer, not a collector or publisher, and for him illuminated manuscripts were a source of inspiration for the creation of new work and not an end in themselves. Nor was he particularly interested in reviving medieval techniques; the new medium of chromolithography was there to be used and it was ideal for the full-colour reproduction of illumination.

As with his earlier illuminated books, such as *The Sermon on the Mount* (1844) and *The Preacher* (1849), the book was designed as a complete work of art. The main text is type-set, but every page has a decorated border – each one different – with a varying amount of hand-drawn text at the beginning of each psalm. The range of colours is somewhat restricted, but the original drawings (which are preserved in the NAL, together with copies of the printed volumes) show that the colours were intended to be much brighter than they appear now. The book is bound in Leake's Patent 'Relievo leather', much favoured by Jones, which allowed for heavily embossed designs – in this case, different designs on the front and back, blocked in blind (see also p. 65). This book, and others like it, were hardly practical, being too large (and, in the case of much of the calligraphy, too illegible) to read normally, but were intended as impressive gifts, suitable for leafing through on a Sunday afternoon. The devotional text, the medieval inspiration, and the modern technology used in their production make them absolutely typical of their time.

THE PSALMS
OF DAVID

Illuminated by Owen Jones (1809–1874). (London: Day & Son 1861).
[6], 13 p., col. ill.
Pressmark: Drawer 99

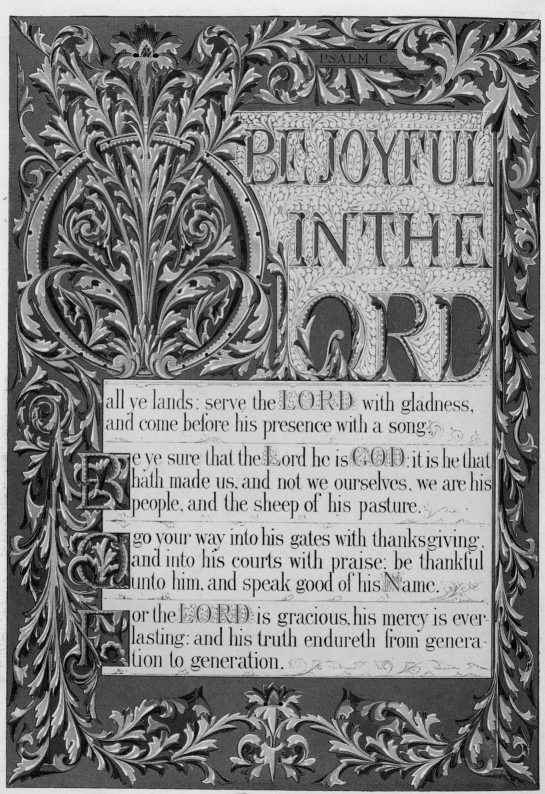

PSALM C.

BE JOYFUL IN THE LORD

all ye lands: serve the LORD with gladness, and come before his presence with a song.

Be ye sure that the Lord he is GOD: it is he that hath made us, and not we ourselves, we are his people, and the sheep of his pasture.

O go your way into his gates with thanksgiving, and into his courts with praise: be thankful unto him, and speak good of his Name.

For the LORD is gracious, his mercy is everlasting: and his truth endureth from generation to generation.

PAGE LXII. DAY XIX.

A GARDEN BY THE SEA

For which I let slip all delight,
Whereby I grow both deaf and blind,
Careless to win, unskilled to find,
And quick to lose what all men seek.

Yet tottering as I am and weak,
Still have I left a little breath
To seek within the jaws of death
An entrance to that happy place,
To seek the unforgotten face,
Once seen, once kissed, once reft from me
Anigh the murmuring of the sea.

THE BALLAD OF CHRISTINE.

Of silk my gown was shapen,
Scarlet they did on me,
Then to the sea-strand was I borne
And laid in a bark of the sea.

O well would I from the World away,
But on the sea I might not drown,
To me was God so good,
The billows bore me up aland
Where grew the fair green-wood.

There came a knight a riding by
With three swains along the way,
And took me up the little one
On the sea-strand as I lay.

He took me up, and bore me home
To the house that was his own,
And there so long I bode with him
That I was his love alone.

But the very first night we lay abed
Befell this sorrow and harm,
That thither came the king's ill men,

A Birthday Present from William Morris

WILLIAM MORRIS
(1834–1896)

A Book of Verse.
With a drawing by
Edward Burne-Jones
(1833–1898) and
miniatures by Charles
Fairfax Murray
(1849–1919). 1870.
[4], 51, [1] p., col. ill.
Accession no.:
MSL/1953/131
Pressmark:
KRP.A.47

This charming work epitomises the multifaceted genius of William Morris. It was his first important venture into the art of illumination, which he took up seriously in about 1870, and there is certainly nothing amateurish about the result. Characteristically, his efforts were preceded by detailed study of manuscripts in the British Museum, going back to the originals rather than relying on the many manuals of illuminating that were being published at about this time.

In accordance with medieval practice, the book was a collaborative effort, helpfully recorded at the end of the volume by Morris in a note dated 'August 26th 1870'. Most of the pictures, including the portrait of Morris on the title page, were by Charles Fairfax Murray, some based on drawings by Morris; but the illustration for the first poem was the work of Edward Burne-Jones. Some of the pattern work was drawn by George Wardle, coloured by Morris, and also all the coloured letters; but 'the rest of the ornament I did, together with all the writing'. Morris composed all the verses, two of which were translations from Icelandic. The book was bound in vellum by Rivière & Son with a design of gold *fleurons* on both covers. This perfect piece shows Morris the poet, Morris the master of ornament, and Morris the maker of fine books.

It is also, in spite of being a collaborative effort, a very personal work which shows Morris the man. The book was made as a

birthday present, the fortunate recipient of which was Edward Burne-Jones's wife Georgiana. Morris and Burne-Jones were close friends, and their families remained close after they both married, but by the late 1860s both Janey Morris and Edward Burne-Jones were having extra-marital affairs. There is no evidence that their spouses followed suit, but it is tempting to see this volume as one result of their common plight.

A facsimile was published by the Scolar Press in 1981.

Edward Johnston's
Book of Sample Scripts

There can be little argument that Edward Johnston was one of the most successful calligraphers of the twentieth century, for this reason: the sanserif typeface which he was commissioned to design for the London Underground in 1913 is still in use today and is instantly recognisable. It has become one of the icons of the machine age, which is perhaps ironic given that Johnston's skill as a calligrapher was firmly rooted in a Renaissance tradition.

The origins of modern calligraphy can be traced back to William Morris, as we have seen, and it was Morris's secretary, Sydney Cockerell, who encouraged Johnston to devote his life to the art. One of Johnston's great achievements was to be able to write in a variety of hands, and this is brilliantly demonstrated in *The House of David, his Inheritance: a Book of Sample Scripts*, commissioned by Cockerell in 1913, completed in March 1914, and presented to the V&A by Cockerell in 1959. It consists of a series of biblical texts relating to King David in Greek, Latin and English, written out on vellum in red and black ink in a variety of scripts. In the colophon, Johnston wrote: 'I record with regret erasures occurring on pp.17.23.27.31. these pp. should have been rewritten but I promised to finish the book by Lady day... The caps on pp.11.12 are not quite happy, but as to a word here and there the Writer nearly is.' A facsmile was published by the V&A in 1966.

Johnston's influence on twentieth-century calligraphy has been enormous, and he may be said to have founded an English school of modern calligraphy. This was partly due to his publications, notably *Writing & Illuminating, & Lettering*, first published in 1906, but also in large part to his teaching: he was appointed to the Central School of Arts and Crafts in London in 1899 and from 1901 taught also at the Royal College of Art. One of his pupils was Eric Gill, for whom he wrote a manuscript Lord's Prayer in about 1913 that subsequently belonged to Heather Child, by whom it was presented to the V&A in 1977.

EDWARD
JOHNSTON
(1872–1944)

The House of David, his Inheritance: a Book of Sample Scripts.
1914.
Parchment.
18 leaves (2 blank).
Accession no.:
MSL/1959/4391
Pressmark: KRP.A.38

your servants : but if I prevail against him, and kill him, then shall ye be our servants, and serve us. And the Philistine said, I DEFY THE ARMIES OF ISRAEL THIS DAY; GIVE ME A MAN, THAT WE MAY FIGHT TOGETHER. And when Saul and all Israel heard those words of the Philistine, they were dismayed and greatly afraid. ——✻——✻——✻——✻——✦

NOW David was the son of that Ephrathite of Beth-lehem-judah, whose name was Jesse; and he had eight sons: and the man was an old man in the days of Saul, stricken in years among men. And the three eldest sons of Jesse had gone after Saul to the battle: and the names of his three sons

11

LUX UMBRA DEI

Light is the shadow of God

SUN   DEFINITIONS FROM THE O·E·D

The brightest, as seen from the earth, of the heavenly bodies,
the luminary or orb of the day;
the central body of the solar system,
around which the earth and other planets revolve,
being kept in their orbits by its attraction
and supplied with light and heat by its radiation.

SUNNE

The feminine pronoun was used
at least until the 16th century
in reference to the sun;
since then the masculine
has been commonly used.

SUNDIAL

A contrivance for showing the time of day
by means of a shadow cast by the sun
upon a surface marked with a
diagram indicating the hours.

THE BIRTH-DAY OF THE UN-CONQUER-ED SUN   **DIES NATALIS INVICTI SOLIS**

Inspiration for this panel came from the delight
in raising six sunflowers from seed. Planted in
April in jiffy-pots on the kitchen window sill,
they stood twelve feet high in the garden in August
and were indeed majestic children of the Sun.
Heather Child scripsit, Spring 1980

Full many a glorious morning have I seen,
Flatter the mountain tops with sovereign eye,
Kissing with golden face the meadows green,
Gilding pale streams with heavenly alchemy

For if such holy Song Entrap our fancy long·Time will run back and fetch the age of gold

Of the Floure of the Sun
or the Marigold of Peru
   From ·THE HERBALL· or General History of Plantes · Gathered by
John Gerarde of London·Master of Chirurgerie ·1636·

DESCRIPTION

The Indian Sun, or the golden floure of Peru, is a plant of such stature and tallnesse that in one summer,
being sowne of a seed in Aprill, it hath risen up to the height of fourteene feet in my garden...
the middle part thereof is made as it were of unshorn velvet, or some curious cloath wrought
with a needle: which brave work, if you do thoroughly view and mark it well, it seemeth to be
an innumerable sort of small floures...when the plant groweth to maturitie the floures
fall away, in place whereof appeareth the seed, black and large...set as though a cunning
workman had of purpose placed them in very good order, much like the hony-combs of Bees.

THE TIME

The seed must be set or sown in the beginning of April, if the weather be temperat, in the
most fertill ground that may be, and where the Sun hath most power the whole day.

THE NAMES

The floure of the Sun is called in Latine Flos Solis... because it resembles the beams
of the Sunne...whereupon some have called it Corona Solis and Sol Indianus:
the Indian Sunne-floure: Chrysanthemum Peruvianum, or Golden floure of Peru:
in English: the floure of the Sun, or Sun-floure.

The Sun in Splendour

Quotations on a theme: the Sun · Sunflowers · Sundials

In heraldry the sun may be blazoned "in his splendour" or "in his glory" – it is represented by a
disc environed with rays alternately straight and wavy – symbolic of both light and heat.

SOLE ORIENTE FUGIUNT TENEBRAE   SHADOWS FLEE AT DAYBREAK

LUCEM DEMONSTRAT UMBRA   SHADOW SHOWS THE LIGHT

SOL REX REGUM   O SUN · KING OF KINGS

HORAS NON NUMERO NISI SERENAS   I NUMBER NONE BUT SUNNY HOURS

IN· SCRIPT-IONS FROM SUN· DIALS

TEMPUS FUGIT   TIME FLIES

ENJOY THE MOMENT   **FRUERE HORA**

TEMPUS VOLAT · HORA FUGIT   TIME HASTENS · THE HOUR FLEES

SURGE ILLUMINARE

SOL OMNIBUS LUCET

The Sun shines for All

The Sun in Splendour

HEATHER CHILD
(1911–1997)

The Sun in Splendour: Quotations on a Theme – the Sun, Sunflowers and Sundials. 1980. Parchment. 1 leaf. Accession no.: MSL/1980/177 Pressmark: Frame store

The Sun in Splendour is a late and, to many people, surprisingly modern example of the work of Heather Child, who was not only one of the most distinguished calligraphers of her time but was also a highly effective promoter and champion of the craft. This piece, which was one of a number of examples of calligraphy commissioned for the exhibition 'The Universal Penman' held at the V&A in 1980, not only demonstrates Child's skill as a calligrapher but also reflects her lifelong interest in flowers, about which she was extremely knowledgeable and which she drew beautifully. This can be seen in the book which she published in 1956, *Collins Pocket Guide to Wild Flowers*, as well as in such unique works as *The Wild Flowers of Ashley and Gowell,* privately commissioned and executed between 1936 and 1939, and which Child bequeathed to the NAL.

Heather Child stands in that important line of descent from William Morris we have already seen: she was a pupil of Mervyn Oliver, who was in turn a pupil of Graily Hewitt and Edward Johnston (Hewitt, like Johnston, was a favourite of Sydney Cockerell). In the words of Nicolas Barker, 'she was the keystone of the bridge that links Johnston and his work with the host of contemporary calligraphers who have spread his lessons, so well exemplified by her, all over the world'.

Her debt to Johnston is acknowledged in one of her most important achievements, the editing of Johnston's *Formal Penmanship*, published in 1971, followed in 1986 by a further collection of Johnston's unpublished papers, *Lessons in Formal Writing*. But she was also able to communicate her skills through her own writing: *Calligraphy Today*, first published in 1963, with revised editions in 1976 and 1988, and *The Calligrapher's Handbook* of 1976, revised 1985. Although she recognised the excitement of the newer school of spontaneous calligraphy, she nonetheless insisted on the importance of practical legibility, a quality which is sometimes overlooked; but she was by no means opposed to innovation, even accepting the role of computers in the craft.

2 Nineteenth-Century Book Illustration

The National Art Library has extensive holdings of illustrated books dating from the fifteenth century, a collection which reflects the practice of the best illustration at the present time and in the past. The nineteenth century is particularly significant in the history of book illustration. As in so many aspects of life, a huge transformation occurred. At the beginning of the century the oldest methods of illustration – woodcut, engraving and etching – were still pre-eminent, but other methods such as wood-engraving and aquatint were being developed. The nineteenth century was one of great flux and experimentation; techniques such as steel-engraving and nature printing (making impressions on paper of natural objects, for example leaves or ferns) appeared, only to be superseded by more enduring methods.

There were a huge number of significant developments and inventions which impacted on the book, including lithography and associated experimentation in colour printing, the invention of photography, and most of all the mechanisation of the entire process of book production. The invention of the steam-powered press, stereotype printing and photography made it cheaper and easier to produce books. The development of circulating libraries and public libraries and the repeal of duties on paper and newspapers all helped to give more people access to reading material that was more affordable than previously, and the rapid rise in the levels of literacy and an increasing population meant that the demand was greater than ever before. Illustrated books and periodicals

played a huge part in satisfying the need for visual stimulus and entertainment in the days before the arrival of cinema and television.

Illustrated material was aimed not just at instructing and entertaining the newly literate through works of fiction, manuals of instruction and weekly periodicals, but also at owners of private libraries who read works on travel, natural history, science, architecture or archaeology. Only they could afford lavishly produced works with lithographed or chromolithographed plates. Lithography, a method of printing from stone, was discovered by Alois Senefelder in Munich in 1798. Initially it was used for printing music, and it was not until the 1820s that it became popular for illustrations. Part of its appeal was that in contrast to woodcuts or copper engraving, the artist could draw directly on to the stone, or on to paper which could then be transferred to the stone. Moreover, many tones of the same colour and almost any kind of paper could be used. However, the problem of integrating text and illustration remained, as the plates, as with copper or steel engravings, had to printed separately from the letterpress.

Chromolithography, a term coined by Gottfried Engelmann for the process patented by him in Paris in 1837, was a development of lithography which outlasted other processes such as those of George Baxter and Charles Knight. It was an elaborate process, requiring up to 20 separate stones and drawings, one for each colour, which were then overprinted one after the other. This technique was used particularly in 'illuminated' gift books, such as

Gray's Elegy (1846) and *Maxims and Precepts of the Saviour* (1848), lithographed by Owen Jones and Henry Noel Humphreys respectively.

Thomas Bewick's development of the technique of wood-engraving during the 1790s was to have a major influence on book illustration in England during the nineteenth century. Wood-engravings were more delicate and could provide a much greater level of details than woodcuts and, unlike copper or steel engravings, they could be printed with letterpress text for books. In his own lifetime, Bewick had only a handful of imitators and pupils and it was not until the 1860s, more than 30 years after his death, that wood-engraving achieved pre-eminence as an illustrative method.

The mid-nineteenth century saw an explosion in periodical publishing. Most of these publications, of which the NAL has a representative selection, combined text and illustration. There were works of instruction such as Charles Knight's *Penny Magazine*, news and satirical publications like *Punch, The Illustrated London News* and *The Graphic,* in addition to religious or 'family' periodicals such as *The Churchman's Family Magazine* and *Good Words*. Publishers deliberately included words indicating the pictorial content in the titles: *The Illustrated Inventor, The Illuminated Magazine, The Illustrated Crystal Palace Gazette, The Pictorial Times*. Many of these periodicals had substantial circulations: *The Illustrated London News* was selling 100,000 copies weekly by 1851, the more literary *Good Words* 80,000 by 1870.

A small number of wood-engravers, such as the Dalziel Brothers, W.J. Linton, and Joseph Swain, produced the highest quality of illustrative work, particularly during the mid-

nineteenth century. The Dalziels engraved the illustrations of Dante Gabriel Rossetti, William Holman Hunt and John Everett Millais of the Pre-Raphaelite Brotherhood in William Allingham's *The Music Master* (1855) and Tennyson's *Poems* (1857). By the 1860s, wood-engraving had achieved its zenith in the work of illustrators such as Arthur Boyd Houghton, George Pinwell, John Dawson Watson and Fred Walker. The Harrod Collection (presented to the NAL in 1933) consists primarily of books and periodicals from this period.

There was then a deterioration in the quality of book illustration. This can be attributed in part to the demand for bigger wood blocks by the illustrated journals, and in part to the increased use of photography. It was now possible to use photography to transfer designs on to the wood block, and the skills of the wood-engraver were rendered obsolete. The line block and half-tone replaced the wood-engraving, the photogravure superseded the engraving, and the collotype and photolithography took the place of the lithograph.

The Private Press Movement which flourished in the 1890s arose partly as a reaction to what was perceived as the commercialisation and mechanisation of book production. The books published by William Morris's Kelmscott Press or Charles Ricketts's Vale Press emphasised quality and craftsmanship in binding, illustration, typography and paper. The last decade of the century also saw the flowering of the Aesthetic Movement, which manifested itself in the illustrations of Aubrey Beardsley for Oscar Wilde's *Salomé* (1894), and in the ground-breaking periodicals *The Yellow Book* and *The Savoy*.

Journal des Dames et des Modes

The *Journal des Dames et des Modes* is one of the outstanding fashion periodicals of the first half of the nineteenth century and remains an important source for the study of fashion for this period. Under the inspired editorship of Pierre de la Mésangère, a former priest and professor of philosophy, the *Journal* provided its subscribers with eight pages of text and at least one hand-coloured fashion plate every five days. The influence of the editor was such that the periodical became known simply as '*La Mésangère*', and he wrote most of the texts himself. The consecutively numbered plates were entitled '*Costume Parisien*', and generally depicted one or two figures in fashionable dress. The earliest plates were rarely signed, except for the occasional mention of the engravers, Voysard and Baquoy, but they are thought to be largely the work of Claude-Louis Desrais with some contributions by Jean-Baptiste-François Bosio. Later artists included Carle Vernet, his son Horace Vernet and Philibert-Louis Debucourt.

The plates produced by these artists and craftsmen were outstanding, not only in their fashion detail, but also in the refinement of their draughtsmanship and delicacy of colour. At the turn of the century the *Lady's Magazine* in England, among others, was copying plates from the *Journal*, although details of the dress were often altered to suit the taste of English readers, who tended to dress more modestly at this time. The standard of illustration set by the *Journal* was never met by other fashion periodicals of the period, and by the middle of the century many English magazines such as

Townsend's Quarterly Selection of Parisian Costumes had ceased producing their own plates, preferring to import plates from the *Journal* with English descriptions.

A German edition of the *Journal* was published in Frankfurt from 1798 to 1848, inspired by that of *La Mésangère*, with the text appearing for a time in both French and German. Another edition was published in Belgium from 1818.

Almost a hundred years later a fashion periodical of the same name was produced by Tom Antongini and Jacques de Nouvion in homage to the artistic excellence and production values of its predecessor. It ran for two years (1912–1914) and itself became a model of visual excellence in the Art Deco style.

1812.

Costume Parisien.

(1214.)

Pelisse Turque, Garnie de Martre.

JOURNAL DES
DAMES ET DES
MODES

Paris: [s.n],
1797–1839.
Pressmark: 42.NN.19

Early Lithography in Britain

In the issue of *The Repository of Arts, Literature, Commerce, Manufactures, Fashions and Politics* for the month of April 1817, Rudolph Ackermann published what is regarded as the first lithographic picture to appear in any journal in Britain. It was taken from a drawing in chalk by Samuel Prout, but the lithographer is unknown. This monthly periodical, which took its name from a print shop established by Ackermann in London in 1795, includes examples of a variety of illustrative forms including woodcuts, stipple engravings, aquatints and lithographs. Several works which first appeared there were subsequently reprinted separately in book form, such as J.B. Papworth's *Rural Residences* (1819) and A.C. Pugin's *Gothic Furniture* (1828). Although it appealed primarily to the female reader with its quality fashion illustrations, it contained something for everyone – sporting prints, poetry, book reviews and articles on science and travel. Before the end of its first year there were no fewer than 3,000 subscribers.

Lithography was introduced to Britain from Germany in 1801 by Philip H. André, brother of the partner of the inventor of lithography, Alois Senefelder. Ackermann was an enthusiast and evangelist for the new method. In 1819 he presented a portable lithographic press to the Royal Society of Arts and also translated Senefelder's treatise *A Complete Course of Lithography*. Unlike the original Munich edition, it contained two lithographic plates – the first lithographic colour printing in England.

Ackermann, born in Saxony in 1764, was a something of a polymath as well as a philanthropist. During his busy life he invented a method of waterproofing paper and leather and adopted the use of gas to light his premises, as well as assisting *emigrés* fleeing political unrest in Europe. He began his working life as a coach designer before coming to London some time in the 1780s. He died in 1834.

Specimen of R. Ackermanns Lithography.

THE REPOSITORY OF ARTS, LITERATURE, COMMERCE, MANUFACTURES, FASHIONS AND POLITICS

(London: Rudolph Ackermann 1809–28). 40v., ill.(some col.). Pressmark: II.RC.R.1-43

Lear's Early Work

EDWARD LEAR
(1812–1888)

Illustrations of the Family of Psittacidae or Parrots: the greater part of them species hitherto unfigured, containing forty-two lithographic plates drawn from life and on stone
(London: E. Lear 1832).
4p., 42 leaves of plates, col. ill.
Pressmark: II.RC.GG.38

Edward Lear, best known today for his nonsense verse and limericks, was also a talented watercolourist with a high reputation as an ornithological illustrator. His *Illustrations of the Family of Psittacidae or Parrots* was the first illustrated book to be devoted to a single family of birds. Unlike most of his contemporaries, who preferred to work with stuffed birds, Lear drew his subjects from life. His work was well received, being compared favourably with John James Audubon's *Birds of America*, the landmark work of ornithological illustration, illustrated with aquatints, which began publication in 1827. It also led to other more lucrative commissions for the aspiring artist; he worked with the taxidermist and zoologist John Gould on a number of the latter's publications, including *A Century of Birds* (1832) and *Birds of Europe* (1832–37). In 1832 Lear was asked by Lord Stanley, later the Earl of Derby, to make drawings of the animals in his private menagerie at Knowsley, near Liverpool. The drawings and accompanying verses he produced for the Earl's children were the basis for Lear's *Book of Nonsense*, published in 1846.

Lear, who was a self-taught artist, set about drawing the parrots in the newly opened Zoological Gardens in Regent's Park in 1830 as a means of earning some money. He had planned to portray every member of the parrot genus and to publish the plates for subscribers, limited to 175, in 14 folios priced at 10 shillings each. However, the expense of paying colourers and printers proved too onerous and only 12 folios appeared. A total of 42 hand-

coloured lithographs were published by Lear in association with Rudolph Ackermann; the lithographs were printed by Charles Joseph Hullmandel, who was largely responsible for the popularisation of lithography in England.

Until this time, lithographs had been primarily used for portraits and landscapes. Lear was one of a few artists who were starting to use the medium for the illustration of natural history. With wood-engraving or engraving, the artist was reliant on the skill, or otherwise, of the engraver, and the risk was that the style and detail of the original would be lost. With lithographs, which involved drawing directly (or in reverse) on to the lithographic stone or plate, the artist had more control over the finished product.

Mr. Pickwick addresses the club.

London: Chapman & Hall, 166, Strand.

Pickwick the Periodical

CHARLES
DICKENS
(1812–1870)

*The Posthumous Papers
of the Pickwick Club*
(London: Chapman
and Hall 1837).
xiv, 609p., [42] leaves
of plates, ill.
Pressmark: Forster
Collection F.48.A.40

The Posthumous Papers of the Pickwick Club, Dickens's first novel, was published in monthly parts from March 1836 to November 1837, and established the author's reputation. The publication of novels in parts dates back to the mid-eighteenth century, but the enormous success of *Pickwick* revolutionised the publication of fiction in Victorian England. Some of the most famous works of Dickens's rivals and contemporaries – William Makepeace Thackeray, William Harrison Ainsworth, R.S. Surtees and Anthony Trollope, as well as those of Thomas Hardy and H.G. Wells – were to appear in serial form, either published on their own as part issues or in magazines such as *Household Words* or *The Cornhill Magazine*.

Pickwick Papers, for all its subsequent popularity, did not have propitious beginnings. Originally it was conceived as a series of sporting sketches – *The Adventures of the Nimrod Club* – by the comic artist Robert Seymour, with the text being subordinate to the illustrations. Dickens had just had *Sketches by Boz* published and was still relatively unknown when he took on and, indeed, took over the project. 'Nimrod' became 'Pickwick' and the first issue appeared in March 1836.

It was not until the publication of the fourth issue in June that sales took off. Seymour had committed suicide after completing three of the four etchings for the second issue and the work of his successor, R.W. Buss, was of a poor standard. Dickens overlooked the established John Leech and a fledgling artist called William Makepeace Thackeray and chose instead the unknown Hablot K. Browne, better known as 'Phiz'. Browne would illustrate Dickens's work for the next 23 years.

With the fourth issue, the number of pages increased from 24 to 32 and the number of plates was reduced from four to two. Due in no small part to Phiz's illustrative style, *Pickwick* became a huge success. From sales of about 500 for the first two parts, 40,000 copies of each monthly part were being sold by the end of 1836. Chapman & Hall, who published the monthly parts, also published *Pickwick* in one volume for 21 shillings in November 1837. According to the publishers, 800,000 copies of various editions of the novel had been sold by 1879.

A Splash of Colour

With the publication of a Christmas supplement with four colour plates printed by George Cargill Leighton in December 1855, the *Illustrated London News* became the first journal in the world to publish colour plates. The supplement sold rapidly and thereafter colour became a regular feature in this and other popular periodicals.

A former apprentice of the colour printer George Baxter, Leighton and his brothers Stephen and Charles Blair took over the colour printing firm of Gregory, Collins & Reynolds in 1849, to form Leighton Bros. The firm was well known for the high quality of their colour printing work, and their illustrations in the *News* were extremely popular: the picture of 'Little Red Riding Hood' sold 100,000 copies. George Leighton was appointed printer and publisher of the *News* in 1858, a post he held until his retirement in 1884.

The *Illustrated London News* was founded in 1842 by Herbert Ingram, a Nottingham printer and newsagent, who later became an MP. Ingram's original idea had been to publish an illustrated paper aimed at a literate audience describing court cases. However, the first issue which appeared on 14 May 1842 had a broader news and current affairs content. With 16 pages and 32 wood-engravings, it cost sixpence and sold 26,000 copies. Early issues reflected the content and style of contemporary illustrated journals, particularly *Punch* and Charles Knight's penny publications. The *News* soon developed its own style and became best known for reporting disasters, wars and state occasions, and by 1863 it was selling over 300,000 copies a week. Rivals and imitators such as the *Pictorial Times* and the *Illustrated Times* appeared on the scene, but Ingram bought them up.

The list of illustrators employed by the *Illustrated London News* reads like a who's who of Victorian art: Sir John Gilbert, John Leech, 'Phiz', George du Maurier, Ford Madox Brown, Myles Birket Foster, Luke Fildes and John Tenniel all contributed. Many artists started their careers with the illustrated popular press which, far more so than books, provided them with a regular source of income.

ILLUSTRATED LONDON NEWS

(London: Illustrated London News Ltd 1842–present).
v., ill.
Pressmark:
PP.10.A–B

CHARLES KNIGHT
(1791–1873)

Old England: a pictorial museum of regal, ecclesiastical, baronial, municipal and popular antiquities (London: Charles Knight 1845).
2v., ill. (some col.).
Pressmarks:
215.G.12-13

Colour Experimentation

Old England, published in 100 parts by Charles Knight (who was also the editor), and printed by William Clowes & Co., was the first book with colour plates printed for the popular market. It portrays primarily the architectural treasures of England, both secular and ecclesiastical, from before the Norman Conquest to the late eighteenth century. The book contains 2,488 uncoloured wood-engravings and 24 colour plates, drawings mostly attributed to T. Scandrett and engravings to S. Sly. These plates were produced by means of what Knight called 'illuminated printing', patented in 1838. Using wood and/or metal blocks attached to a rotating table, it was possible to print one colour after the other (up to a total of 16) on to the paper. This method had the advantage of significantly reducing the labour involved in producing quality colour prints.

Charles Knight worked as a journalist before founding the Society for the Diffusion of Useful Knowledge with Henry Brougham in 1828. Knight was first and foremost dedicated to educating the masses through publishing cheap illustrated books and magazines. The most successful of these was the *Penny Magazine*, published between 1832 and 1845. By the end of its first year it had a circulation of 200,000, though it faded in the 1840s as a result of competition from magazines which included sensational fiction and crime reports.

As a colour printing technique, illuminated printing was one experiment among many which did not endure. It remained the practice to print each sheet one colour at a time, waiting until each colour was dry before printing the next. Unlike a contemporary of his, George Baxter, who also patented a method of colour printing, Knight had no licensees. Because of the complexity of the technique, no one else took up his patent and it was used in only a handful of his own publications.

Chromolithography

The Industrial Arts of the Nineteenth Century was the most ambitious chromolithographic project of its time. In a postscript to his introduction, Matthew Digby Wyatt described the book as 'the most important application of Chromolithography to assist the connection which should subsist between Art and Industry which has yet appeared; and further, … it has been produced upon a scale of magnitude, and with a degree of rapidity, unexampled in this or any other country'. It was one of the last books of its kind to be produced 'by hand', without the intervention of photographic reproductive techniques.

The Industrial Arts was conceived as a means of reproducing the best examples of design shown at the Great Exhibition of 1851. Wyatt selected the objects, collaborated closely with the artists and lithographers, and wrote the descriptive text. The work appeared fortnightly in 40 parts between October 1851 and March 1853, in an edition of 1,300 copies. In the latter month it was also published in five sections, each comprising eight parts, and in two volumes. As each colour needed a separate impression, each plate required an average of seven separate printings; one even required 14. According to Wyatt, in order to keep pace with the demand, the work was pulled through the printing press no fewer than 18,000 times a week, amounting to 1,350,500 pulls. It required 1,069 lithographic stones, weighing a total of 25 tons, and consumed 17,400 lb of paper for the plates alone.

Wyatt, who was primarily an architect, first came to prominence in 1849 when he was selected by the Society of Arts to visit Paris with Henry Cole to write a report on an exhibition of French industrial products. Consequently he was appointed Secretary to the Executive Committee of the Commissioners for the Exhibition of 1851 in London. There he won prize medals for his designs and received a gold medal from Prince Albert for his services to the Exhibition. Around this time he worked with Isambard Kingdom Brunel in designing Paddington Station and with Owen Jones in designing the Fine Arts Courts at the Crystal Palace, Sydenham. Knighted in 1855, he was appointed the first Slade Professor of Fine Art at Cambridge in 1869.

MATTHEW DIGBY WYATT (1820-1877)

The Industrial Arts of the Nineteenth Century: a series of illustrations of the choicest specimens produced by every nation, at the Great Exhibition of Works of Industry, 1851 (London: Day and Son 1851–53). 2v., col. ill. Pressmarks: 49.E.11-12

Art and Ornament

OWEN JONES
(1809–1874)

*The Grammar of
Ornament* (London:
Bernard Quaritch
1868).
1v. in 2 (157p.) ill.
(some colour)
Pressmarks:
G.58.A.11-12

First published in 1856, with 100 folio plates drawn on stone by Francis Bedford and printed by Day & Son, Owen Jones's *The Grammar of Ornament* is one of the masterpieces of nineteenth-century chromolithography. It was the first time that so many illustrations of ornament from so many countries and periods had been represented in colour in one work. *The Grammar of Ornament* was issued in 10 parts, selling at 14 shillings each and the bound volume at £19.12.0. Later the same year a 'new and universal' quarto edition with 12 additional plates was published in 30 parts at 3s.6d. each. This was subsequently re-issued by Quaritch in 1868. The plates, which were made directly from Jones's hand-coloured drawings, were accompanied by text by Jones himself as well as J.O. Westwood, J.B. Waring and Matthew Digby Wyatt.

Jones, who had trained as an architect, developed an interest in Arabic form and ornament while visiting the Alhambra at Granada in 1834. This inspired him to produce his detailed drawings of the decoration of the palace in *Plans, Elevations, Sections, and Details of the Alhambra*, published in two parts in 1836 and 1845. As he could find no firm to carry out colour printing to his requirements, Jones, in association with the lithographers Day & Haghe (later Day & Son), set up his own press. In the pre-photographic age, chromolithography was the only means of attempting a faithful representation of such ornamental details. During the 1840s, Jones proceeded to use chromolithography to produce 'illuminated' gift books, imitating the style of illuminated manuscripts from the Middle Ages.

As Superintendent of Works of the Great Exhibition of 1851, Jones played an important part in decorating and arranging the Crystal Palace. The following year he was appointed joint director of the decoration of the Crystal Palace when it moved to Sydenham. He also began lecturing at the Department of Science and Art, founded by his friend Henry Cole at the South Kensington Museum. Cole assisted Jones in formulating his philosophy that ornament should be based on geometry, and saw that *The Grammar of Ornament* could be used as a means of spreading knowledge of the collections at the Museum. It has proved to be a remarkably influential and enduring work, and is still in print as well as having been recently issued as a CD-ROM.

The Dalziels and Wood-Engraving

The Parables of Our Lord, with illustrations by John Everett Millais engraved on wood by the Dalziel Brothers, is one of the most important illustrated books of the period. The engravers suggested the project to the artist in 1857 but it took over six years for the completion of 20 out of the 30 projected illustrations.

The Dalziels were familiar with Millais's work from the mid-1850s, when the firm engraved many of his drawings, such as those for Anthony Trollope's *Orley Farm* and *Framley Parsonage* which appeared in various serial publications. In 1857 the Dalziels engraved the work of Millais and his fellow Pre-Raphaelites Dante Gabriel Rossetti and William Holman Hunt for Tennyson's *Poems*, published by Moxon. Millais, in accepting the commission for *The Parables*, described it as a labour of love. The length of time it took to complete the work was explained by the artist in a letter to the Dalziels:

> I can do ordinary illustrations as quickly as most men, but these designs can scarcely be described in the same light – each Parable I illustrate perhaps a dozen times before I fix and the 'Hidden Treasure' I have altered at least six times.

Millais's skill and patience was appreciated by the Dalziels and the critics, if not by the public. A reviewer in the *Athenaeum* wrote in December 1863 that the majority of the designs possessed 'high qualities of art'. In 1862, 12 of the illustrations were printed in the weekly family magazine *Good Words*,

before the entire series was published by Routledge in 1864, but like many illustrated gift books of this nature it was not a commercial success. For Millais, *Parables* led to greater things – he was elected to the Royal Academy in 1863 and later acquired great popularity as a portrait painter.

Primarily wood-engravers, the Newcastle-born Dalziels (brothers George, Edward, John and Thomas, and sister Margaret) were also artists, printers and publishers. They were the most influential and successful firm of engravers of the period. Their work encompassed almost every major illustrated book published in Britain from 1840 to 1890 and included engravings for Edward Lear's *Book of Nonsense* (1862) and John Tenniel's drawings for Lewis Carroll's *Alice* books (1866 and 1872).

THE PARABLES OF OUR LORD AND SAVIOUR JESUS CHRIST

(London: Routledge, Warne and Routledge 1864).
[12], 48p., 20 leaves of plates, ill.
Pressmark: Harrod Collection 55.B.40

The Hidden Treaſure.

Photography as Art

PETER HENRY
EMERSON
(1856–1936)

*Pictures of East Anglian
Life* (London:
Sampson, Low,
Marston, Searle and
Rivington 1888).
150p., xxxii leaves of
plates, ill.
Pressmark: 51.C.36

These photographs and those in Emerson's
seven other books of photographs published
between 1887 and 1895 succeeded in changing
the way photography was perceived in the
late-nineteenth century. In the preface,
Emerson stated that he aimed to 'produce
truthful pictures of East Anglian peasant &
fisherfolk life'. The photogravures were etched
on copper and were 'with one or two excep-
tions, untouched, so that they may be relied
upon as true to Nature'.

Emerson was to become one of the first
photographers to promote photography as an
independent art. In his *Naturalistic Photography
for the Students of Art* (1889), he maintained
that photographs should be direct and simple,
showing people in their own surroundings as
they were, and not dressed up as models in a
studio. In advocating this view, Emerson was
challenging figures in the photographic establishment such Henry Peach Robinson and Oscar
Rejlander. He wanted photography to be
regarded as an art in its own right, different
from, though neither superior nor inferior,
to painting.

It is no coincidence that on the title page
of *Pictures of East Anglian Life*, Emerson uses a
quotation from Jean-François Millet, one of
the painters of the Barbizon School, who
painted realistic scenes in open air. In his zeal
to promote his ideas on photography, Emerson
presented portfolios with the best images from
the book to every British and foreign photographic society. Although he was soon to reach
the conclusion that photography was a very
limited art, as he outlined in *The Death of*

Naturalistic Photography (1890), Emerson started
an important debate on photography. He is
also regarded as forerunner of the purist
approach dominant in photography in the
United States from the 1920s.

Emerson, a distant relation of the American
writer Ralph Waldo Emerson, trained as a doctor. He began to photograph in 1882 as an aid
to the anthropological study of rural life in East
Anglia. Though not a socialist (he was later to
advocate polygamy and education only for the
few), Emerson's pictures and commentary in
Pictures of East Anglian Life were regarded by
some of the book's subscribers as an attack on
the existing social order. Painters were more
complimentary; John Collier said of the photographs that they were 'wonderfully true to
nature' and James Charles described the
ploughing picture as 'a poem'.

3 Bindings

The book as we know it today is technically known as a codex. The word is derived from the Latin for tree trunk, an interesting parallel with the origin of the word 'book', which is generally believed to have come from the word for 'beech'. Why these words are associated with the tree is still much debated.

The codex came into existence in Rome in the third century BC, when clay writing tablets were joined together by thongs. By the first century BC, tablets had been replaced by membranes or sheets of parchment. The codex gained in popularity, providing most cheap and portable books by the first century AD. The scroll, however, remained the chief means of distributing text throughout the Roman period. Early Christians popularised the codex, and, made from papyrus leaves, it was much used by them in Alexandria.

The rise of Christianity brought the codex growing prestige. The scroll became associated with pagan writings and by the late fourth century AD had almost completely been displaced. The codex developed further. With the use of parchment and paper, large sheets were folded over to create two leaves. When inserted one into another and stitched, the folds gave greater strength to flexible but structurally weak materials like paper.

In Europe the invention of printing from movable metal alphabetical types had an immense impact on book production. Texts could now more easily be produced in multiples and all the book-related trades expanded, including binding.

From medieval times, when books were written out by hand, up to the early nineteenth century, it was usually either the bookseller, or the buyer directly, who undertook to send books to the binder. The sheets would be delivered from the scriptoria or printing office, loose or loosely stitched. For ordinary readers the trade binding of plain calfskin or sheepskin over boards was adequate to protect the text. For the wealthy collector a richly designed cover, possibly with the mark of ownership imparted by a coat-of-arms stamped in gold, was an important adjunct. The letters of St Jerome with their references to jewelled bookbindings show that richly bound books were objects of importance at least as early as the fourth century AD.

The origins of the title and later half-title page were as covering leaves. Early Italian printers left the first page blank to protect the text before it was bound and by the 1470s an abbreviated title was printed on this page for ease of identification. By the middle of the sixteenth century such title pages had become very elaborate and carried much information about the title, author, contents, printer and bookseller. This led in the seventeenth century to the title in turn being protected by means of a further blank leaf, which itself during the eighteenth century began to be printed with an abbreviated title, the half-title.

The sheets of text were folded and the folds of each gathering of pages stitched. Using a sewing frame it was possible at the same time to pass the stitching round cords which then ran across the spine of the text-block. These cords were used to attach the board and allowed them to be flexibly hinged. Large books for public and ceremonial use were originally bound in wooden boards, but since the sixteenth century most books have had boards made up by pasting paper or straw together to make up paste boards and straw boards. This process completed the basic binding; however, it was usual to cover the book with leather, pasting it down firmly on to the spine and boards.

The craft of bookbinding has not changed for centuries but the appearance of the book has changed often. The coverings were of various leathers but chiefly vellum or a dark brown calf. By the late sixteenth century, tanning techniques allowed the production of coloured leathers, mainly red, blue and green.

The decoration of book bindings is most likely of Arabic origin. While some binding decoration was done in Byzantium and in medieval Europe, the modern European tradition originates in Italy whence it came from Byzantium through the trading city, Venice. In north Italy gold leaf was used with heated tools to produce impressed gilt designs. Among the tools used was the large panel stamp, a stamp often nearly as large as the book cover. By the mid-sixteenth century it was common in Europe to use small hand-held tools in combination to create a variety of designs, often symmetrical. The fillet or roll also came into widespread use allowing a continuous line or repeating design to be built up. All these tools are heated before application and can be used in blind (i.e. blank on to the leather) or with gold leaf to create a gilded design. Surface patterns can also be produced by onlaying pieces of leather of different texture or colour, or alternatively inlaying pieces in recesses.

In the early 1820s a London binder first made the experiment of covering part of an edition in cloth, and from then on book-cloth gradually replaced leather. The rise of the publisher or publishing partnership separated from the role of bookseller, and the development of industrial techniques in the book trade all acted together to increase the number of complete editions given uniform bindings.

Early cloth was weak in structure and unattractive. To overcome the lack of strength and the buying public's resistance, book-cloth was treated to provide resilience and to make it appear not unlike traditional bindings. This was done by the impregnation of gum-arabic which created buckram, and a substantial amount of cloth was patterned with grains resembling morocco leather and later small pebbles and other patterns.

Towards the end of the nineteenth century hand-binding gave way to machine-binding – or what should more correctly be described as casing. The traditionally bound book has boards firmly attached to cords or thongs as described above. The cased book by contrast has a prefabricated case of cardboard covered by cloth or paper glued on to the text-block under pressure. The modern hard-cover is invariably cased and the results can be surprisingly strong if good-quality glues and materials are used.

The appearance of paper dust jackets seems to have paralleled the use of cloth bindings. In the last quarter of the nineteenth century they became common and illustrations appear along with blurbs and publishers' advertisements.

The paperback is a twentieth-century phenomenon but has antecedents in the wrappers used to cover books and pamphlets from the early days of printing. Plain and printed papers, marbled and paste, have all been used to provide protection to the text-block but also to give the book a pleasing exterior. As with dust jackets, the paperback wrapper has become an important vehicle for illustration, advertising and much innovative cover design.

Through all periods the talents of a wide range of artists besides the bookbinder have been drawn to the book: the illustrator on both text and binding, also the jeweller and embroiderer. In the twentieth century *livres d'artistes* were produced by artists famous in the traditional fine arts and in the last decades of the century book art (see Chapter 8) had its influence on the design of bindings both traditional and avant garde to be published in the twenty-first century. The following examples from the Library's European collections have been chosen to give a flavour of the variety of designs and changes of fashion that have come into existence over the last 500 years. The invention has been almost infinitely versatile, but always working within the strict confines of the form which the codex lays down.

A Florentine Binding of the Late Fifteenth Century

MARCUS TULLIUS
CICERO
(106–43 BC)

*De Amicitia. c.*1460.
Parchment. 39 ff.
213 x 132 mm.
Humanistic script in
Latin.
Accession no.:
MSL/1951/937
Pressmark: KRP.A.27

Gospels written on papyrus in the monasteries of the Coptic Church in Egypt in the first centuries of the Christian era were bound as codices and given leather bindings. These were decorated by tooling, incising and the addition of onlays or jewels. The examples surviving from the ninth and tenth centuries show designs with decoration drawn from the Hellenistic tradition, a tradition bequeathed to us from the medieval world by way of the Roman Empire.

Islamic bookbinding originated in the skills developed in Christian Egypt and Syria. The sweeping conquests of expanding Mohammedanism absorbed this craftsmanship and transmitted it across North Africa and into Europe through Sicily and Spain.

Fifteenth-century Europe saw rapid changes in the commercial production and distribution of manuscripts and printed books. Rising literacy and increased interest in the works of classical Greece and Rome expanded demand by private individuals for books decoratively bound. To meet rising production, techniques changed. The large panel stamp and the roll tool producing a repeating pattern were introduced. The last change in technique in the fifteenth century was the introduction of gilding in Italy, again adopted from Islamic craftsmen. The influence of their use of materials, techniques and styles was strongly felt in Europe.

Italy was pre-eminent in the art of bookbinding in the late fifteenth century and the example shown, dating from the last decades of the century, illustrates the sophistication

achieved in design and execution. The binding is chiefly tooled in blind but with subtle use of gilt roundels to give a sumptuous effect. Apart from the early use of gold tooling, the patterns of the design illustrate clearly the influence of the Orient. The interlaced cablework, the star and the roundels are common motifs on bindings of the period, as also on other bindings the almond shape.

Cicero's *De Amicitia* was one of the influential works of classical Roman moral philosophy much studied in Europe from Renaissance times. Many manuscript copies were produced until the economic benefits of printing supplanted commercial scriptoria. As with most innovations, printed copies were to begin with looked down upon as not quite as good as the manuscript. Early printed books therefore copied both the script and design of traditional manuscripts – an influence which has lasted into present times.

A Seventeenth-Century English 'Centre- and Corner-Piece' Binding

Printing and bookselling in England, chiefly carried out in London, experienced rapid growth in the seventeenth century. The demand for bindings led to growth in the trade-binding sector as well as a desire for fine and decorated bindings. The difference between the trade and the commissioned binding was in the fineness of the materials used and the extent and skill in applying decoration.

The trade binding was basic and functional with little decoration apart from a panel formed by plain fillet tooling. For a small extra charge the tooling could be executed in gold and the appearance enriched. The unique binding made for a particular client's book would use the best-quality materials in the stitching. The boards were often thicker and heavier and covered by unblemished and well-tanned leathers, richly dyed. But the chief difference was aesthetic. Gold tooling and lettering decorated the covers and spine, page edges were gilt, and silk-covered bands embellished and strengthened the head and tail of the spine.

Edward Gwynn, who commissioned the binding illustrated, was a lawyer who died in 1649. He was an enthusiastic book-collector and regularly had his name lettered in gold on the covers of his books. Most surviving examples from his library are much plainer than this, but here he celebrated a manuscript, probably of his own compilation, bringing together a select number of Acts of Parliament. The bindery he chose was prominent in London at the time and bindings attributed to it are often said to be by the 'squirrel binder'

after a particular tool which the firm very often employed.

The style of the binding is known as 'centre- and corner-piece'. Derived from the Islamic use of sunken panels, it was widely used throughout Europe in the late sixteenth and early seventeenth centuries. Quite often the centre-piece used was the coat-of-arms of the book owner and was either the sole mark of ownership, or as here, a further celebration of the owner's pride in his collection.

MEDULLA PARLIAMENTIS

1622.
Paper. 366 ff.
(10 blank).
364 x 225 mm.
English.
Accession no.:
MSL/1948/1774
Pressmark: CLE N9

Eighteenth-Century Scottish 'Herring-Bone'

ROBERTUS
EWART

*Dissertatio medica
inauguralis, de scrofula*
… Edinburgh: apud
T. W. Ruddimannos
1749. 23 p.
Pressmark: Drawer 6

Many and various famous styles have developed over the centuries of European binding: for example, 'Lyonese', with geometrical strapwork coloured by painting, lacquering and enamelling; 'centre- and corner-piece'; and, in the sixteenth century, 'fanfare', using small tools to create geometric circular and oval shapes, the spaces between filled with sprays of foliage and decoration.

In Britain the late seventeenth and eighteenth centuries saw a golden age in bookbinding. The Restoration of King Charles II stimulated an artistic renaissance. The 'cottage' style is seen on many fine bindings – a gilt or painted ornament formed like a roof gable placed at the top and bottom of the covers. *Pointillé* – employing small tools to create complex naturalistic patterns – and two ornaments, the one based on the Ionic capital (but commonly known as the 'drawer-handle') and the double-handled vase, were frequently used. Many of the best bindings of the period are associated with the King's binder, Samuel Mearne.

These developments were precursors to the splendid flowering of binding styles in Dublin and Edinburgh in the second half of the eighteenth century. In Scotland two distinctive national styles emerged: the 'wheel', formed of two fans placed back to back at the centre, and the 'herring-bone', formed of a vertical central stem with branches sprouting at regular intervals. As in the beautiful example illustrated, holly leaves were a common motif. Made in about 1750, this medical treatise is bound in brown morocco with very fine gold tooling using a variety of small ornaments and *pointillé* work. The nationality of the style is emphasised by the use of coroneted thistles. Edinburgh's medical schools were of international renown and many treatises published by teachers and students were published and bound in the city.

French Jewelled Book of Hours

Some of the most beautiful books made have been prayer books. The medieval church appointed seven hours in the day for the saying of prayers and these were seen as central to personal religious devotions. For those with worldly means much artistic effort was expended on creating beautifully illuminated manuscripts as an aid to devotion, an offering of beauty to God, and of course an expression of wealth.

The example illustrated here is modelled on the supreme achievements of the high Gothic. There was a growing revival of interest in Gothic, that is medieval, arts in the nineteenth century, and this book is an early instance of that interest passing from the collection of medieval artefacts to the emulation of medieval artistic achievement. Louis Jules Gallois, Comte de Naives, commissioned the work in 1828 as a gift for his wife, Adèle, who sadly died in 1837 before its completion.

The extensive colophon gives a detailed account of the book's manufacture. Twenty-two painters took 14 years to complete the illumination while one scribe took 10 years to write out the text. The miniatures were painted by Charles Leblanc and Auguste Ledoux. Folios two and three were added in 1850 and the book was bound by the King's Binder, Alphonse Simier. The prayer book was then taken to Rome and blessed by Pope Gregory XVI.

The binding is reminiscent of the richly embellished bindings that were once created for church and royal use and display. The boards are covered with precious metal and enchased by jewels created by François Mellerio. Clasps keep the text-block of vellum leaves firmly pressed and the edges of the leaves are richly gilt.

HEURES FRANCOISES ET LATINES POUR MADAME L. GALLOIS

1828–50.
iv, 127 leaves.
Accession no.:
MSL/1987/7
Pressmark: Safe 2.B.1

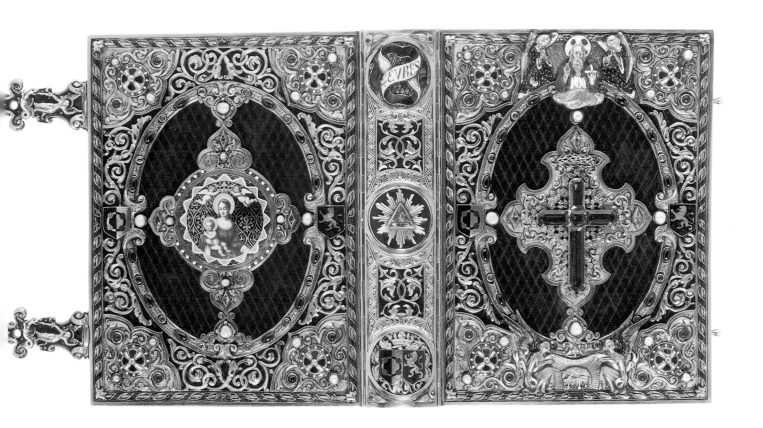

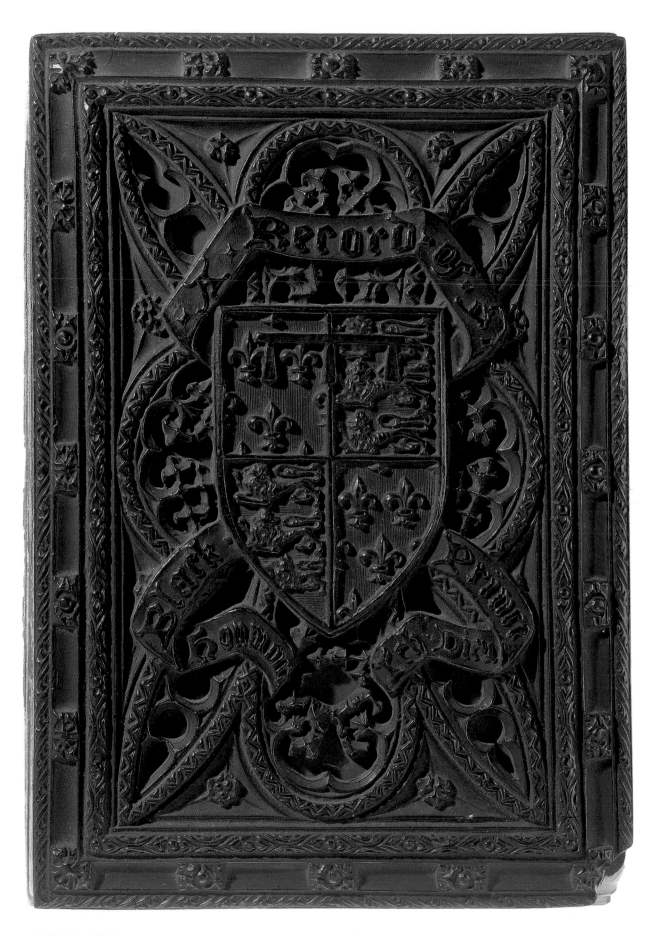

English *papier mâché* of the 1840s

HENRY NOEL
HUMPHREYS
(1810–1879)

*A Record of the Black
Prince* (London:
Longman, Brown,
Green and Longmans
1849).
xciv, ii p., col. ill.
Pressmark:
Drawer 69

Paper was experimented with, and used quite widely, as a binding material in the Victorian period. Many beautiful and striking book covers resulted but generally their importance is in the printing techniques used. But paper was also used as moulded *papier mâché*. Mixed with plaster of Paris and possibly also antimony, the moulding was done on a stiff frame, often metal. Mainly black, the designs chiefly had a medieval flavour in keeping with the spirit of the Gothic Revival. Striking effects were achieved by lattice work showing a red or metallic underlay. The process was patented by the firm Jackson & Sons, who manufactured almost all examples known. Many were designed and executed by Henry Noel Humphreys, including the example illustrated. The final binding of the book, using a leather spine, was undertaken by trade binders such as Leighton.

Similar effects were achieved by relievo bindings which used the traditional material, leather, which was softened and then moulded and deeply embossed. The patent was held by a firm called Leake but the binding was carried out by the trade binders Remnant & Edmonds. Owen Jones, famed for his Gothic designs and ornament, was closely involved in the production of designs for relievo bindings. Other materials were used and experimented with to produce bindings in high relief and with novel effects – wood, vellum, various textiles, porcelain, paper, and enamelling, to name but a few.

Henry Noel Humphreys was one of the most important book designers of his time. He was active in many fields of the book, as author, illustrator, illuminator as well as designing book covers. He is known for his use of the Gothic style in such elements as black-letter type, foliage and borders. His covers are never signed and attributions depend often upon his authorship, connection with the book or knowledge of his style.

The example illustrated was written by him, and he notes that in creating the design, he took one of the compartments of the Black Prince's tomb in Canterbury Cathedral as his model. This explains the authentic feel of the book as a fitting memorial to the Prince's life, a sense which is increased by the medieval style of the design and illustration of the printed text.

English Cloth Binding, 1864

The cloth binding was introduced so that publishers could provide the bookseller, and in turn the book buyer, with a ready-bound book at reasonable cost. It took both time and money to take stitched quires to the binder, but if that was not done a book was soon damaged by ordinary use.

In the 1820s binding cases were developed to replace traditional binding. The case was prefabricated in bulk and attached to the text-block by pasting the outer endleaves on to the inner covers. A piece of cloth was used to strengthen the spine. As various processes were progressively mechanised, economies of scale developed and it became cheaper to bind as much of the edition as possible, even though it was only in the twentieth century that the process was finally fully mechanised. Since cloth is stronger than paper, and cheaper and more abundant than leather, cloth cases swiftly became accepted. This was especially so as by the 1830s cloth was being embossed, and an easy method of stamping gilt decorations on covers had been discovered. The use of decoration overcame resistance to the drab appearance of plain cloth bindings with paper labels. The process of blocking book-cloth-covered boards with large gilt and coloured designs required the design and engraving of stamps which were impressed using powerful steam presses.

John Leighton, who sometimes used the pseudonym Luke Limner, was a book illustrator and designer of bookplates and book covers, also achieving some fame as a writer. He was a member of the family bookbinding firm Leighton Son and Hodge which was the dominant force in the production of excellently designed pictorial cloth bindings in the late nineteenth century.

In 1852 Leighton published *Suggestions in Design*, in which he maintained that contemporary style did not exist but that authority was obtained from the distant past. He laid down various propositions which provided his governing principles for construction, decoration and colour. A very similar exercise was conducted by Owen Jones in his *The Grammar of Ornament* in 1856 (see p. 51).

The cover design illustrated shows much similarity with other Victorian art, most particularly the Gothic Revival, and follows some basic precepts: it is decorative, regular and geometric, uses conventional representation, and is two-dimensional in plane surfaces. Leighton used symbols, particularly heraldry, and motifs illustrative of the work's content. Within the symmetrical layout he employed panels of a variety of shapes, ovals and rounded corners being favoured, and a number of intersections of double shapes.

Issued in both red and blue cloth, this is a case binding of morocco grain cloth over bevelled paste boards. The gold design is panel-stamped in gold and blind (without colour) and signed 'JL' (i.e. John Leighton). The sumptuous effect is finished by gilding the book edges and the use of cream endpapers. Most copies still contain the binder's ticket on the lower pastedown which reads 'Bound by Leighton Son and Hodge'. The market for such extravagantly produced volumes, extensively illustrated, on heavy paper and richly bound, arose from the custom which flourished in the Victorian age, of giving beautiful editions of classic works of literature as presents.

DANIEL DEFOE
(1661?–1731)

The Life and Adventures of Robinson Crusoe (London: Routledge, Warne and Routledge 1864). xx, 497, [1] p., ill. Pressmark: 55.B.36

Matisse, Bonet and *Jazz*

HENRI MATISSE
(1869–1954)

Jazz (Paris: Tériade
1947).
146, [9] p., col. ill.
Pressmark:
Safe 1.D.3

©ADAGP,
Paris and DACS,
London 2000

Matisse, the painter and sculptor, also produced several important *livres d'artistes*, an art form which attracted a number of modern artists in the twentieth century, most particularly after the Second World War. He espoused Expressionism and described his composition as 'the art of arranging in a decorative manner the various elements at [his] disposal'. His stated intention was 'to reconcile man to himself by means of aesthetic harmony'. *Jazz* was completed late in his life but is very evocative of his paintings and shows his love of colour and joyousness. Freshness and spontaneity is achieved by producing the text and accompanying illustrations directly from the lithographic stone. The colours used in the plates are bright, basic and fully saturated, and these are mirrored by the binding.

Paul Bonet is one of the twentieth century's great binders, both in skill of execution and creativity of design. He began his career as a fashion designer but, influenced by the noted book artist, Paul Legrain, turned to bookbinding. As the binding of *Jazz* demonstrates, Bonet was emotionally sympathetic to Matisse's Expressionism. However, he was also able to turn his fantasy-rich technical skills to the service of the Cubist and Surrealist styles when required.

This binding, made in 1952, acts as an introduction to the book's visual content but is in no way repetitive or derivative. Bonet achieves his own highly individualistic use of colour. Rather than working towards an effect to be achieved on the open pages of a book, his canvas is the solid quarto volume.

The basic brown calf binding is but a small part of the whole once the full conception has been achieved. Comprising a complex pattern, the cover is created from coloured leather inlays, shaped pieces of leather inserted to replace the original of exactly the same shape. Despite the use of different leathers, this results in a smooth surface, not possible with the alternative method of onlaying. Rather, the intricacy of Bonet's design means he is working at a mosaic, and the great number of joins are finished with consummate skill by delicate fillet gilding.

A Book Wall

The traditional craft of bookbinding, which at its finest results in a work of art, individual and aesthetically decorated, experienced a revival in the latter half of the twentieth century. A major impetus was the establishment of the association of craft binders called Designer Bookbinders. Originally called the Guild of Contemporary Bookbinders, this organisation has encouraged the arts of the book since the 1950s. An early member of the Guild, Philip Smith became one of the most prominent names in fine craft book-binding and was President of Designer Bookbinders in 1977–79.

Smith's work encompasses both the traditional format of the book as well as the avant garde fields of book art and book sculpture. His bindings make great use of onlays and inlays, often in intricate patterns and producing visually exciting graphic designs. Maril, a special technique of inlaying thin split leather veneers with marbled finishes, was developed and patented by the artist.

The Bible was printed at the Doves Press by Thomas James Cobden-Sanderson and Emery Walker. The Doves Press, working in the tradition of William Morris and his Kelmscott Press, was established by T.J. Cobden-Sanderson, a successful barrister, who abandoned the law to set up a bindery and then printing press purely to produce excellence in book production, and to provide satisfying work for himself and colleagues, rather than for any commercial motive. He was a follower of the philosopher Spinoza and wished to emulate him by living a life of aesthetic simplicity and working with his hands. In collaboration with Emery Walker he developed a type that would be associated with the Doves Press alone. They took Nicolas Jenson's type of 1476, the type which lay behind Morris's 'Golden Type', and revived it in its true Roman form. The paper used at Doves Press was supplied by Batchelor's of Little Chart, the company that had supplied the Kelmscott Press, and it was watermarked with Cobden-Sanderson's design comprising two doves and the initials of the two men.

This copy of the Doves *Bible* was bound in five volumes in 1977 and is representative of Smith's craftsmanship and artistic abilities. Each of the bindings has a distinctive design, but they are interconnected so that the set can be stood together to form a panorama or, in the words of the artist, a 'book wall'. Smith uses the bindings to express his vision of the world's creation as formed by primordial and cosmic forces.

THE ENGLISH BIBLE: CONTAINING THE OLD TESTAMENT & THE NEW

(Hammersmith: Doves Press 1903–05). 5 v.
Pressmarks: X950087-91

Bond in Paperback, 1964

The term 'paperback' refers to more than a binding. In a commonly accepted definition it is a book of more than 96 pages (shorter works are called 'pamphlets' or 'brochures') with paper or thin card wrappers. The binding is adhesive and 'perfect', meaning that the leaf folds are cut to provide a perfectly thin and flat face on to which the wrappers are glued. The price of a paperback is generally relatively low and it is produced in large print runs. Use of a small typeface size, narrow margins, low-quality paper, a standard size and the payment of low royalties all help to maintain low production costs and thereby to achieve high-volume sales at a low price.

Paper covers had been used since at least the sixteenth century, but the history of the paperback really begins with Tauchnitz Verlag, a German publishing firm which produced a series of English-language reprints from 1841. By 1939 they had published over 8,000 titles, and with austere printed wrappers had established the major features of the cheap paperback which was marketed chiefly through railway bookshops.

In Britain in 1935, Allen Lane began his series of 'Penguins'. These sold for sixpence each and were available, not in bookshops, but from Woolworths' stores. Within two years seven million copies had been sold and in 1937 the firm started the 'Pelican' imprint for serious non-fiction, many of which were commissioned originals. Wartime paper rationing helped in gaining acceptance for this cheap type of publication and by 1965 over 100 million books had been produced by about 30 publishing firms.

In the United States of America, publishers developed the glossy, brightly coloured, eye-catching wrappers. Penguin was slow to adopt pictorial covers, but when they did, maintained a high standard of artistic design, commissioning graphic artists like Peter Bentley who, through cover designs, created a visual identity for Evelyn Waugh's fiction.

Pan Books were more aggressive in the market place and achieved success for their more populist fiction with offset printed laminated covers in four or five colours. This paperback edition of Ian Fleming's very popular James Bond spy novel makes use not only of the visual techniques to attract people to buy the book, but also exploits the popularity of the film of the book. The film-star Sean Connery's face is immediately recognisable and the girls in revealing clothing promise that the sex appeal of the film is also to be found in the book. The cover title reads as if the text were the start of a film and most strikingly the cover is actually die-cut to imitate the sprocket holes of film strip.

IAN FLEMING
(1908–1964)

From Russia with Love
(London: Pan Books
1959)
(1964 printing).
207 p.
(Pan Books; X236).
ISBN 0330102362
Pressmark:
SN 92.0086

4 Documentary Manuscripts

Documentary manuscripts – by which we mean unpublished material whose importance lies primarily in its content rather than in any aesthetic value, although it may possess that too – can be found in every corner of the V&A's estate. Like any other institution, the Museum is constantly generating records of its own activities, and as these activities relate to the acquisition, care and display of objects, the records can often be of great documentary value to those with an interest in art and design. The V&A Archive and Registry (responsibility for which was assumed by the NAL in 1993) is very much more than a resource for the study of the V&A. Because of the role played by the Museum, particularly in its early days, it has much to tell about the history of design and education in this country, and about the history of the art market, collecting and dealing. Departmental archives also contain much valuable material, and the Theatre Museum Archive is of paramount importance in the field of the performing arts.

For the purposes of this work, however, we are concerned with those manuscripts which the Library has acquired from outside the Museum, with a view to supplementing its holdings of published works. Indeed, little distinction was at first made between published and unpublished material: they were stored in the same way and catalogued according to the same rules. The important place of manuscripts within the Library – which had been collected since its foundation – was confirmed by the bequest of John Forster in 1876, which included not just the manuscripts by Swift and

Dickens discussed below, but also correspondence of David Garrick (some 1,600 letters) and Samuel Richardson, and a remarkable collection of autographs. The Leonardo notebooks also formed part of the Forster Bequest, and to some it would seem perverse to categorise them under so mundane a heading as 'documentary manuscripts'; to Leonardo, they were but a stage in his thought process, and it is only to subsequent generations that they have acquired value as objects in their own right.

The Forster Bequest was exceptional, in terms of its size, subject matter, and quality. For the most part, the manuscripts collected by the Library related closely to its expected interests. The papers of artists predominate, especially those of the nineteenth century and the first half of the twentieth: correspondence (ranging from single letters to many hundreds), diaries, ledgers, notes and drafts for books published and unpublished, by artists, designers, dealers and scholars. Among artists represented, Ford Madox Brown is included here, but many others might equally have been: Edwin Landseer, John Everett Millais, George Romney, or John Constable, for example. The records of the Bond Street art dealers J. Smith and successors, 1812–1908, illustrate another aspect of the art world. The documentation by scholars of art and design in all its aspects – church armour, medieval wall paintings, Arabic glass weights, enamelled croziers, and merchants' marks, to select five at random, as well as painting and sculpture – which may be all the more interesting for never having been published, constitutes a very large part of the collection, notably the notes and drafts for Crowe and Cavalcaselle's histories of painting, notebooks and papers of W.H.J. Weale on Dutch and Flemish art, and P.W. Reynolds's 84-volume collection of manuscripts, notes, pamphlets, articles and press cuttings on European military costume of the eighteenth and nineteenth centuries.

From the 1930s, manuscripts were increasingly purchased for their documentary value, and at about this time they were brought together within the Library and treated as a separate collection. The major change, however, came in 1978, with the setting up by Sir Roy Strong of the Archive of Art and Design (AAD). This was established in response to fears that certain groups of material were at risk either of being turned away altogether by the Museum, or of damage being done to them by being split up between Museum departments along the established materials-based divisions. A prime example of such an archive is that of Heal & Son Ltd. Consisting of textile samples, administrative files, designs and printed documents, there was no logical place within the Museum to house this material, but to divide it between the Library, Prints and Drawings, and Textiles would have greatly reduced its value to researchers.

The Heal's archive was in fact one of the first to be taken in by the AAD, which now contains over 300 groups. Although these tend to be large — usually very much larger than the groups of material in the main collection of manuscripts — size is not the deciding factor. Rather, what matters is the archival nature of the group, usually representing the *Nachlass* of the firm or individual, where the value of the whole may be greater than its component parts. In line with professional archival prac-

tice, each group is retained and catalogued as an organic unit (whereas in the past a group of letters might have been separated and catalogued under the individual authors or recipients), and is likely to contain a wide variety of media. This last point is well demonstrated by Eduardo Paolozzi's Krazy Kat Arkive, which is hardly an archive in any normal sense of the word, but is included here because, rather like Leonardo's notebook, it shows what lies behind the artist's work.

The emphasis of the AAD is upon the twentieth century, although it does include some important archives which stretch back well into the nineteenth, such as those of the stained-glass manufacturers James Powell & Sons, and Heal's. Subject strengths include textile and fashion, furniture, stained-glass, metalworking, graphics, book illustration, exhibition design, crafts, and interior design. Fine art and sculpture are left mainly for the Tate Gallery, and architecture to the Royal Institute of British Architects, both of whom have active collecting policies in their respective fields.

The NAL continues to acquire both archives and smaller groups of manuscripts, but within ever-increasing constraints. In the past, the problem was often that of rescuing archives before they were thrown out; now, almost everything has a commercial value, and much of what comes on the market is beyond our means. Archives also take up a great deal of space (which is usually why they are discarded in the first place), and that is another commodity of which there is an acute shortage. The computerisation of the Library's catalogue, however, will at least ensure that the many manuscripts already in the Library's collection will become known to an even wider audience.

Notebook by Leonardo da Vinci

The V&A holds three of the notebooks that Leonardo da Vinci kept throughout the second half of his life, in which he recorded ideas, observations, experiments and sketches. Until the middle of the nineteenth century, Leonardo was best known to most people as a painter. It was not until extracts from his notebooks and manuscripts began to be published, followed by facsimile editions, that the full breadth of his interests was made known to a wide audience. The contents are incredibly diverse, including sections on hydraulics, geometry, mechanics and architecture. A few of the notebooks contain detailed investigations of a single subject (one of those in the V&A is devoted to problems in solid geometry), but most contain miscellaneous notes on a wide range of subjects.

The notebooks held by the V&A date mainly from the period Leonardo spent in Milan, where he had moved in about 1482 hoping to gain a position at the Ducal court. In a letter of self-recommendation to the regent, Ludovico Sforza, he outlines those skills he thinks would be of most value. Curiously, he stresses military engineering, mentioning his abilities as an artist almost as an afterthought. He carried out a number of commissions for Ludovico, including a portrait of his mistress, organising pageants, planning an equestrian statue of his father, Francesco Sforza (a long-running project which was never realised), and painting the *Last Supper* in the refectory of the Monastery of Santa Maria delle Grazie. Some pages in the notebooks can be related to particular projects (sketches of horses may represent studies for the equestrian statue, and a floor-plan of Milan Cathedral may date from the time when he was preparing his submission to a competition to design a dome for the cathedral), while others reflect Leonardo's insatiable scientific curiosity.

The page shown here gives a design for a perpetual motion machine with notes in Leonardo's characteristic mirror writing. Over a number of pages, Leonardo investigates the possibility of such a device, sketching three, but finally concluding, 'Oh speculators on perpetual motion, how many vain projects in this search you have created! Go and be the companions of the searchers for gold.'

LEONARDO, DA VINCI (1452–1519)

Notebook.
Milan 1495–97. 1 v.
Pressmark:
Forster MS. 141/2

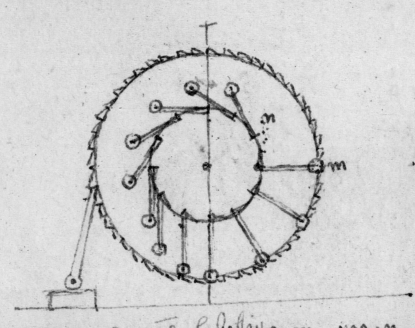

quarta ce: quado la ballotta. m. era un
n quato piso ri stava piu dlada dal polo ce
dqda emfura. essmaj ce iaro eno quar
dare ce io dle madua. qosi bi: de inpo
ce va lero lodo inre to dsmerle epu
te qolle suo prudo: doui tratta d moto e
dpesasoni. ancora seni parla apino

Questa adono de intrali strumen sia igno
rantj gh parra ceallj dluci simple inpo
ce hesso hra sio lego prima unpoce od
moto ce: ce hessa ma ringa alquanto da
ss unpoco d moto ce: de sagiongaa lool
po cinto hisso ce olpo facilment manti
re il prinapato moto eno ce e no stra

I see no creature, I cannot read ... by candle-light. Sleeping will make me sick. I reckon my self fixed here: and have a mind like Marechall Tallard to take a horse and garden.. I wish you a merry Christmas. and expect to see you by Candlemas. I have walked this evening again, about 2 miles on the rocks, my giddyness God be thanked is almost gone, & my hearing continues; I am now retired to my Chamber to scrible or sit humdrum. The night is fair, and they flatter to have some hopes of going tomorrow.
Sept. 26
Thoughts upon being confined at Holyhead.
If this were to be my Settlement during life, I could amuse my self ~~by forming some~~ a while by forming some conveniencyes to be easy; and should not be frighted either by the Solitude, or the meaness of lodging, eating or drinking.. I shall say nothing upon the suspense I am in about my dearest friend; because that is a case extraordinary, and therefore by way of amusement, I will speak as if it were not in my thoughts, and only as a passenger who is in a scurvy unprovided comfortless place without one

without one companion, and who therefore wants to be at home, when he hath all conveniences ^there proper for a Gentleman of quality. I cannot read at night, and I have no books to read in the day. I have no subject in my head at present to write on.. I dare not send my linnen to be washed for fear of being called away at half an hours warning. and then I must leave them behind me, which is a serious point.: in the mean time I am in danger of being lousy, which is a ticklish Point. I live at great expense without one comfortable bit or sup.. I am afraid of joyning with passengers for fear of getting acquaintance with Irish. The Days are short, and I have five hours at night to spend by my self before I go to bed.. I should be glad to converse with Farmers or shepherds, but none of them speak English. a Dog is better company than the Vicar, for I remember him of old. What can I do but write every thing that comes into my head.. ~~to be~~ Watt is a Booby of that Species which I dare not suffer to be familiar with me, for he would ramp on my shoulders in half an hour.. But the worst part is my

Dean Swift's *Diary*

JONATHAN SWIFT
(1667–1745)

Private Diary. 1727.
1 v.
Pressmark:
Forster 48.D.34/10

The name of Jonathan Swift, Dean of St Patrick's Cathedral, Dublin, will be associated in most people's minds with that of his most famous creation, Lemuel Gulliver. The collection of 18,000 volumes bequeathed to the V&A by John Forster is rich in great names. Leonardo da Vinci and Charles Dickens feature elsewhere in this book; Forster also owned a Shakespeare first folio, and a large quantity of letters and manuscript material relating to the actor David Garrick. No less a name is that of the author of *Gulliver's Travels*.

One of Forster's last projects, on which he was working at the time of his death, was a biography of Swift. He was correcting the proofs of the first volume during his final illness; this was published shortly before he died on 1 February 1876, and the work remained incomplete. In preparation for the biography he collected material relating to Swift, including Swift's copy of Alexander Pope's *Dunciad* (inscribed by the author to 'Jonath. Swift, 1729, amicissimi autoris donum'), a copy of *Gulliver's Travels* with Swift's manuscript corrections, and various manuscripts associated with or written by Swift.

Among the latter are notebooks which Swift used to record accounts of private income and expenditure between 1702 and 1741. They include details of all kinds of domestic expenses – food, clothes, horses, and servants – as well as details of money received from the deanery and weekly collections taken in St Patrick's. There are notes about his movements between Ireland and England, and lists of letters sent and received. A single vol-ume of his private diary also survives, begun in Chester on 22 September 1727; it was, in Forster's words, 'written on his way back to Dublin amidst grave anxiety for Esther Johnson [Stella] then dangerously ill'.

The notebooks form an incomplete sequence – there are some years missing – and they do not include any direct evidence of his literary activities, but nonetheless they provide an important window into his life and habits, and a fascinating insight into the minutiae and vicissitudes of daily life in the eighteenth century.

The Goods and Effects of the Late Sir Andrew Fountaine Knight Deceased

Sir Andrew Fountaine was one of the leading connoisseurs of his day and at his Norfolk seat, Narford, he assembled what is now regarded as one of the most celebrated and intriguing of all eighteenth-century collections. This inventory was drawn up at Fountaine's death by Captain William Price, his nephew and heir, and it constitutes a major source for our knowledge of Fountaine's collection and its display at Narford.

One interest of the inventory is the evidence it provides of the way in which the pictures in the house were hung, and the page shown here describes the contents of the 'New Room at the West End', including a portrait of Sir Andrew 'in his own Hair' and a group portrait by Giulio Pignatta painted at Florence in 1715 of Sir Andrew with his travelling companions, Price among them. Another lies in its detailed listing of the library of a formidably learned antiquarian: the inventory is a working copy used by later owners of the collection and it shows how the library was reorganised after Fountaine's death.

Fountaine was a collector, antiquarian and patron of the arts, who developed the study of numismatics in England and assembled a great collection of Italian majolica. Much of his collecting was done when touring on the Continent, but he was hardly typical of the aristocratic Grand Tourist in the range of his interests and the depth of his learning: he was a friend and correspondent of Leibnitz and Cosimo III de Medici, among others. The unpublished poems and manuscripts of Jonathan Swift, which he acquired through his friendship with Swift, were preserved at Narford and used by John Forster when he was working on his *Life of Swift* (see above, p.81).

Two copies of the inventory were made; another remains in the family's possession. Although its importance lies principally in the documentation of a great collection of works of art that has now been dispersed, it also has great charm (as well as historical value) in simply listing the contents of a large house, so that the *objets d'art* are interspersed with mundane household effects, just as they were in Fountaine's lifetime.

ANDREW
FOUNTAINE
(1676–1753)

An inventory of the goods and effects of the late Sir Andrew Fountaine knight deceased at his late house at Narford in the county of Norfolk [and] A catalogue of the library together with the manuscripts &c. at Narford.
[c. 1753].
1 memorandum book
([120] p.)
Accession no.:
MSL/1996/5
Pressmark: 86.ZZ.160

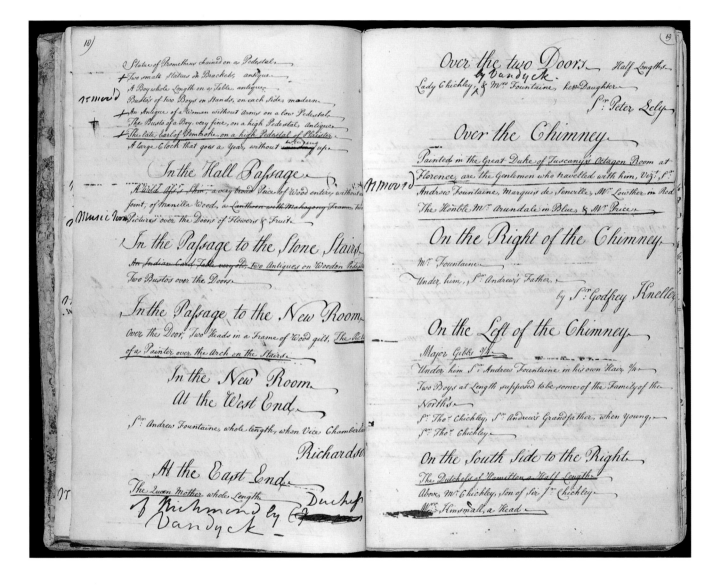

18

Statue of Prometheus chained on a Pedestal
+ Two small Statues on Brackets, antique
+ A Boy whole Length on a Table, antique
remov'd Busto's of two Boys on Stands, on each Side, modern
+ An Antique of a Woman without Arms on a low Pedestal
The Busto of a Boy, very fine, on a high Pedestal, Antique
+ The late Earl of Pembroke, on a high Pedestal of Plaister
A large Clock that goes a Year, without winding up

In the Hall Passage

A Wild Ass's Skin, a very broad Piece of Wood entire without a
Joynt, of Manilla Wood, a Lanthorn with Mahogany Frame, two
Music two Pictures over the Doors of Flowers & Fruit

In the Passage to the Stone Stairs

An Indian Card Table very old, two Antiques on Wooden Pedestals
Two Bustos over the Doors

In the Passage to the New Room

over the Door, Two Heads in a Frame of Wood gilt, The Picture
of a Painter over the Arch on the Stairs

In the New Room
At the West End

Sr. Andrew Fountaine, whole length, when Vice Chamberlain
Richardson

At the East End

The Queen Mother whole Length — Duchess
of Richmond by ~~~~
Vandyck —

19

Over the two Doors — Half Lengths
by Vandyck
Lady Chichley, & Mrs. Fountaine, her Daughter
Sr. Peter Lely

Over the Chimney

Painted in the Great Duke of Tuscany's Octagon Room at
Remov'd Florence, are the Gentlemen who travelled with him, Viz. Sr.
Andrew Fountaine, Marquis de Seneville, Mr. Lowther in Red
The Honble Mr. Arundale in Blue, & Mr. Price

On the Right of the Chimney

Mr. Fountaine
Under him, Sr. Andrew's Father
by Sr. Godfrey Kneller

On the Left of the Chimney

Major Gibbs ¾
Under him Sr. Andrew Fountaine in his own Hair ¾
Two Boys at Length supposed to be some of the Family of the
North's
Sr. Thos. Chichley, Sr. Andrew's Grandfather, when young,
Sr. Thos. Chichley

On the South Side to the Right

The Dutchess of Hamilton a Half Length
Above, Mr. Chichley, Son of Sir Jno. Chichley
Mrs. Kinsmall, a Head

Pugin's Vision

'The present state of architecture is deplorable. Truth reduced to the position of an interesting but rare and curious relic.' So reads Pugin's diary entry for 8 November 1835, sounding a clarion at the outset of a career as the principal practitioner and theorist of the Gothic Revival in English architecture. This extraordinary career is detailed in 15 pocket diaries, covering the years 1835 to 1851, which form only part of an extensive collection donated by his descendants.

The chief source for Pugin's early life is the volume of autobiographical notes made in about 1831. These document his theatrical interests which led him to spend a season at Covent Garden as a stage carpenter. A sketchbook containing notes and drawings of stage machinery suggests the practical design knowledge he acquired at this time. But Pugin turned from the theatre in favour of architecture as the material expression of spiritual truth. This mental process is recorded in a remarkable series of designs undertaken prior to his conversion to Catholicism in 1835. These 'ideal schemes' freely allowed his theatrical imagination to recreate the splendours of the medieval world and to reintegrate artistic expression with religious belief.

Pugin lacked formal training and was considered an outsider in his profession. As a means of practical education he employed his natural facility for drawing. Whether travelling incessantly by rail in pursuit of commissions or making annual tours of the Continent, he filled his sketchbooks with detailed studies of medieval buildings that provided the scholarly

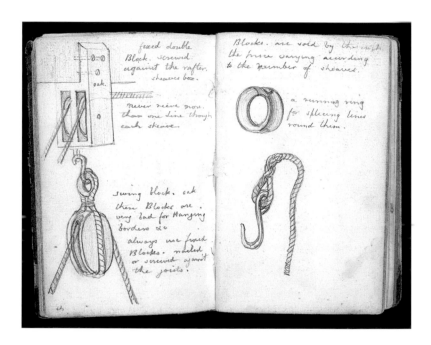

foundations for his own designs.

Although prolific as an author in propagating his beliefs, Pugin's approach was primarily visual, as shown by the volumes of drawings for his books *Gothic Furniture* (1835) and *Contrasts* (1836). The former proved widely influential despite its lack of text; the latter has been considered one of the most original works of the century, a polemic against modern architecture which imaginatively used illustration to provide a direct contrast between medieval glories and contemporary degradation. Pugin's vision inspired the later artistic and social criticism of Ruskin and William Morris; it endures today as an appeal to a design aesthetic based on authentic principles.

AUGUSTUS WELBY
NORTHMORE
PUGIN (1812–1852)

Pocket sketchbook of stage machinery and architectural details.
1831–35.
57 leaves, ill.
Accession no.:
MSL/1969/5198
Pressmark: 86.MM.38

Dickens at Work

CHARLES
DICKENS
(1812–1870)

*Dealings with the Firm
of Dombey and Son.*
[1848].
2 v.
Pressmarks:
Forster 47.A.19-22

The manuscripts of Charles Dickens are perhaps the most celebrated items in the collection bequeathed by John Forster, the novelist's friend and biographer; as such they were kept on display as a public attraction until 1935. They include all but two of the surviving drafts of his novels which, alongside corrected proofs, letters, journalism and miscellanea, document 33 years of Dickens's creative processes. Taken together with the Library's holdings of the original serial parts, first editions and collected editions, they offer an unrivalled resource for the study of his work from conception to publication.

Dickens published most of his novels in monthly parts, valuing an intimate relationship with a responsive audience in spite of the extreme demands this placed on his powers of invention. By mid-novel he was working to a tight schedule, rarely more than a number ahead of his readers. Each month he needed to produce 32 pages of printed text and detailed instructions for two engravings, send the copy to the printers and then correct the proofs. The early manuscripts show Dickens keeping pace with his fluent imagination; but from *Dombey and Son* (1846–48) onwards, the smaller handwriting and continual amendments show him striving to maintain a balance between the design of the novel and the improvisation of each individual number. This developing sense of artistic unity is recorded in his Number Plans, the folded sheets he used to note chapter contents and decisions as to themes, characters and plot.

Dickens never made fair copies of his drafts; they were sent to printers experienced in reading his difficult, heavily corrected script. He then read his proofs with careful haste (sometimes assisted by Forster), and cut the 'over-matter' he habitually wrote to ensure a full number's worth, and which is now uniquely preserved in his manuscripts. A recent conservation project has revealed some 500 pages of cancelled text and has identified changes of nib and ink which further our knowledge of the extent of Dickens's revisions, sustaining his claim to recognition as a conscious and deliberate artist rather than the purveyor of those loose, baggy monsters decried by critics of the Victorian novel.

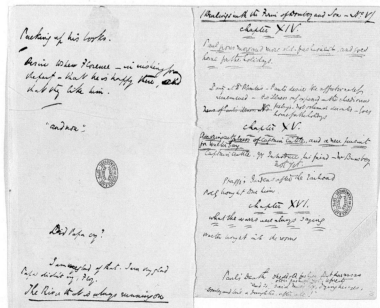

Half Quarter Day

returned from Tunbridge Wells by train
Building: Dilke & the Prince did not wish
Job he told of his plan for disposing of the
Surplus — enjoined them not to tell me.
Reid appd to Governorship of Malta — Queen & Prince
said they regretted his absence: Called on him
in the Ey to discuss University plan.

---- **12 TUESDAY** [224–141] ----

Drawing up Distribution announcement
Building. dined there. with Reid, Dilke, Northcote
Playfair, Cubitt to Southampton by train.
— Sore throat & out of Sorts.

to Archaeological Societies "Commercial": moving them
& governing them by the Statistical Society — In Town
about 9.40. Home with Reid & Dilke. — Cubitt came
to advise about Water Supply &c.

---- **13 WEDNESDAY** [225–140] ----

At Southampton: went to see the Ordnance Map
Office — Engraving by Machinery & Steam: Fairy Steamer
came to fetch us — At Osborne at 12. left at 5.30
Prince proposed to devote the Surplus to Centralising
all the Societies opposite Crystal Palace — & buying
the ground for 50.000 at once. wd make 4 institutions
1 for R.Map. 1. Machinery. 1. manuf: 1 Fine Arts —
governed by Chairmen of each & the Statistical Society —
Discussed. Albert — 4 institution into 1 — Omitted Society
by name — General idea approved. but universal
Condemnation of details — Reid thought it quite imperative
& every laughed at the idea of making the Antiquarian

Home physicking — & writing questions to Phipps
about the Princes Scheme — Fanny
brought Tizby back from Wendover: at
Building. All concurred strongly against the Princes plan
Reid thought it wd be a great misfortune if he published it
& it wd tend to injury the Monarchy — Playfair had suggested
a College of arts & manufactures which Reid assented to —
Arles Defour brought the Mayor of Lyons to ascertain if the
international relations already established wd be
Kept up. — Dined at Home.

---- **15 FRIDAY** [227–138] ----

with Tizby to Royal Academy. — Soc: of arts: Barclays
Chapmans agreed to go on with another Volume of J of
Drays: Building— Ellerton dismissed on charge of taking
Money at the Doors & keeping it — Reid went to Gloster Shire.
Macdonald impatient at Princes silence at others services—
Lloyd & he wanted to be knighted — & not take his wife back
to the Mauritius — Home. In the Ey posting up Diary &c

---- **16 SATURDAY** [228–137] ----

Building. Reid away: Dilke left. Cubitt remarked
on Brunels incurring £200 expense for experiments
for the Iron Dome without authority — Dined at
building. In the Ey with Owen to see Macbeth
at Sadlers Wells. performed according to the original
text & extremely well done. Walked home.

Met Sheepshanks in the morning who wd present
me with the wine not consumed on the Picture day

The Indefatigable Henry Cole

SIR HENRY COLE
(1808–1882)

Diaries, 1822–34,
1837–54, 1856–82.
43 v.
Accession nos.:
MSL/1934/4117-4159
Pressmarks:
Cole Collection
55.AA.02-44

Sir Henry Cole was one of those multitalented indefatigable Victorians, a public servant whose achievements included developing the Penny Post, creating the modern Public Record Office, masterminding the Great Exhibition of 1851 and, last but not least, founding the South Kensington Museum, including what is now the V&A. In his spare time, under the pseudonym Felix Summerly, he published the first Christmas card, and through his *Journal of Design and Manufactures* sought to promote and improve design in manufactured products.

For 60 years he kept a diary, and in it he recorded the changes in attitudes and in practical life that took place between 1822 and 1882. He knew every prominent politician of his day – Lord Derby, W.E. Gladstone, John Bright, Richard Cobden, to name only a few. His own tastes were artistic and early on he made friends with many painters, including Mulready, Millais, Redgrave and Lawrence. Among writers, he knew W.M. Thackeray and T.L. Peacock best, but he was on friendly terms with Dickens, as well as journalists and editors and newspaper proprietors. Musicians, scientists, architects, soldiers, scholars, photographers, clergymen – there is hardly an aspect of nineteenth-century life that was not familiar to him. He travelled throughout Europe, was Prince Albert's right-hand man in organising the Great Exhibition, and was on friendly terms with the whole Royal Family.

Diaries for 57 of those 60 years survive, a total of over a million words. Cole was above all a practical man. He normally wrote five or six lines a day, recording his movements and meetings. On 13 August 1851, the entry for which is shown here, he attended a meeting at Osborne where Prince Albert outlined his plans for spending the surplus from the Great Exhibition, ideas which would lead to the formation of the museums area of South Kensington. This momentous occasion is recorded concisely and factually. There is little introspection, and the diary has no literary merit. What it does offer is a review of almost the whole career of a successful, middle-class, middle-income man and his family.

Ford Madox Brown Turns the Corner

The collection of some 2,000 items relating to Ford Madox Brown, consisting mainly of letters written to him, offers a vivid portrait of an influential yet underrated British painter set against the rich and various background of Victorian society. It allows us to follow the pattern of his career, his sympathy for his impoverished fellow artists and his wary encounters with dealers and critics. Here is the letter which announced a turning point in his fortunes, the Liverpool Academy £50 prize awarded in 1856 for *Christ Washing Peter's Feet*. Brown's leading patrons, drawn from the ranks of provincial businessmen, are all strongly represented, including Thomas Plint of Leeds who commissioned *Work*, Brown's most ambitious painting. This provided the centrepiece for his pioneering one-man exhibition held in 1865 and expresses his deeply felt artistic and social principles. His independence of mind is reflected in the letters of Holman Hunt, most faithful of the Pre-Raphaelite Brotherhood and ally in opposition to the malign influence of the Royal Academy. Brown's later years were dominated by his labours on the murals for Manchester Town Hall and these are well documented through dealings with obstructive councillors, loyal assistants, the architect Alfred Waterhouse, and local luminaries such as C.P. Scott, legendary editor of the *Manchester Guardian*.

Brown's correspondence reveals the broader canvas on which he was engaged. Whether teaching at the Working Men's College, designing *King Lear* for Sir Henry Irving, or playing host to Stéphane Mallarmé and Joaquin Miller ('the Buffalo Bill of Poesy'), he vigorously conducts us across the Victorian panorama of soirées and debtors' prisons, sketching parties and scarlet fever. While poverty and death overshadow many of the lives traced in this collection, the abiding theme is that of remembrance. Recorded here are Brown's efforts in support of the Memorial to Rossetti, his greatest friend; so too his promotion of his son Oliver's literary remains, a tribute to brilliant promise denied fulfilment. After Brown's own death his papers were collected as material for the biography by his grandson Ford Madox Ford; they remained in the hands of his descendants until 1995, when they were acquired by the Library in commemoration of an artist and his age.

JAMES PELHAM
(1800–1874)

Letter to Ford Madox Brown (1821–93).
18 September 1856.
Accession no.:
MSL/1995/14/80/1

18 Sept 1856

6 Marsden Street
Low Hill
Liverpool

Dear Sir

I beg to forward you a
Seven days Sola bill of Exchange
on the Bank of England for Fifty
Pounds being the amount of the
Academy's Prize awarded to you
for your Picture "Christ washing
Peter's feet" now in the Liverpool
Academy's Exhibition —

Your Picture "The last of England"
would have taken the prize if you
had not sent the other, but the
Academy feel greatly obliged
by your kindness in sending the number
you have, Mr Windus and
Mr Robertson wished me to ask
you one question and if you have
the slightest objection to answering
it I hope you will say so. for both
of them would be sorry to intrude
in any way, They want to know
what Vehicle you paint with, if
a Compound in what proportion,
if it convenient to you to say they
would esteem the favour —

If you will be so obliging
as to let me have an answer
to this by return of post, it will be
doing a Service to

Your Most Obed Servt
James Pelham
Sec y

To
Ford Madox Brown Esq

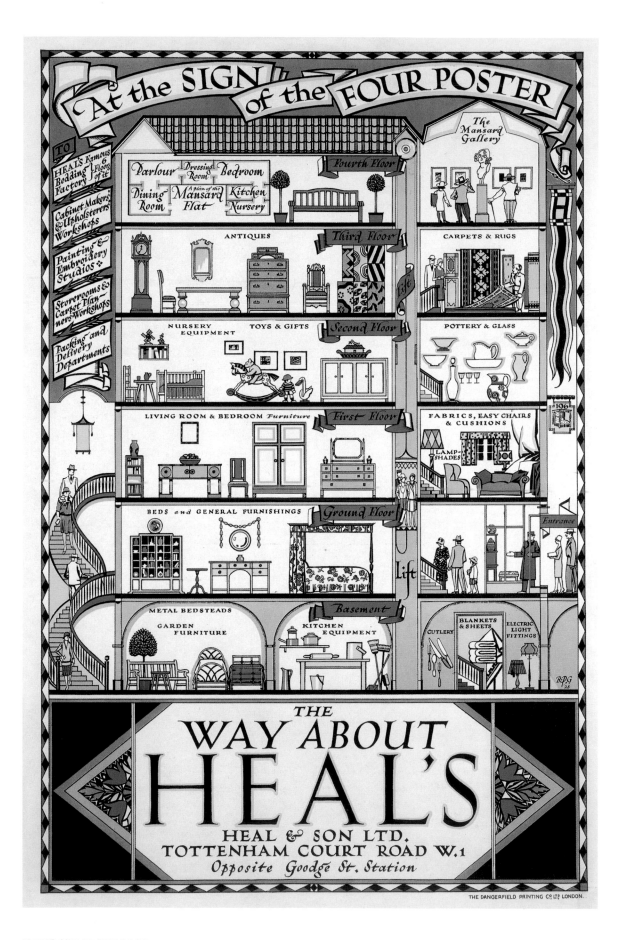

At the Sign of the Four-Poster

HEAL & SON

Heal & Son Holdings
plc: Records.
1810–1995.
c. 4,000 files and
c. 18,750 negatives.
Pressmarks:
AAD/1978/2;
AAD/1986/1;
AAD/1994/16;
AAD/1996/8;
AAD/1997/4;
AAD/1997/13;
AAD/1999/7.

The advertising power of posters was fully exploited at Heal's. R.P. Gossop's poster *At the Sign of the Four-Poster – The Way About Heal's* (1928) conjures up an attractive and inviting pictorial map of the department store. Gossop leads the elegantly dressed shopper from the garden furniture in the basement past the colourful displays of fabrics, household furniture and kitchen wares and up to the Mansard Flat and Mansard Gallery on the fourth floor. This was opened in 1917 as an art and design gallery and was used as a showcase for launching Heal's latest designs.

The family firm of Heal & Son Ltd was established in 1810 as a feather-dressing business. From 1818, when the business moved to Tottenham Court Road, it was known as a mattress and feather-bed manufacturer. In the mid-nineteenth century the company branched into furniture, and pioneered a new idea in shop display in creating the 'room set', which enabled the customer to make the visual leap from product to environment. By the end of the century it ranked among the best-known London furniture houses.

Under the leadership of Sir Ambrose Heal, who joined the firm in 1893, Heal's became renowned for promoting modern design in Britain by encouraging and employing talented young designers who worked in the modern idiom. Sir Ambrose had a keen sense of publicity and expanded Heal's promotional activities. He commissioned the leading graphic artists, illustrators and photographers of the day to design catalogues and posters. Heal's became known for its simplicity and good craftsmanship and by the 1930s was selling house packages of 'Heal's style'.

In 1941 Heal's Wholesale & Export Ltd, later called Heal's Fabrics Ltd, was established to export all Heal's merchandise. Heal's Contracts Ltd was set up in 1944 and undertook furnishing contracts for institutions and organisations. By 1965 the shop had 21 departments divided into three main groups: furniture, soft furnishings and domestic equipment. Sir Terence Conran acquired Heal's in 1983, but in 1990 the firm was the subject of a management buy-out, and it is still trading from its landmark building in Tottenham Court Road.

Degenerate Art

What looks at first to be an unexciting office typescript contains the answer to some of the questions now being asked about the Nazi era: what happened to so many works of art, examples of so-called *Entartete Kunst*, which were seized by the Nazi authorities and subsequently disappeared?

Entartete Kunst means 'degenerate art', and the inventory lists works of art which the Nazi regime in Germany removed from public galleries and museums because they were deemed subversive. Artists outlawed in this way included Marc Chagall, Lovis Corinth, Otto Dix, Max Ernst, Paul Gauguin, George Grosz, Paul Klee, Oskar Kokoschka, Henry Moore, Edvard Munch and Pablo Picasso. Their works were taken from public collections across Germany, originally to gather material for the *'Entartete Kunst'* exhibition in Munich in 1937. These and other works were then disposed of in various ways. Many were sold through foreign dealers, the most valuable in Switzerland, but the sums realised were often derisory. Others were exchanged for works by German Romantic painters, which were more acceptable to the Nazis. At least one painting, by Gauguin, is recorded as entering the collection of Hermann Goering. In 1939, anything that had not been sold was destroyed in a bonfire of nearly 5,000 paintings, drawings, watercolours and prints.

Details of what items were removed from each gallery and what subsequently happened to them were meticulously recorded. 16,558 items are recorded on 480 pages of typescript, arranged according to the town and museum or gallery from which the works were taken. Three copies of the first volume of the list are in other collections, but this is the only known copy of the second volume, covering galleries in cities whose names begin with letters G–Z. Although the full story will probably never be known, this new document adds greatly to our knowledge of what happened to thousands of works of art of which the Nazi regime disapproved.

The list was discovered among a collection of German books and periodicals of the 1920s and 1930s put together by the London art dealer Harry Fischer and given to the Museum by his widow in 1996.

GERMANY. REICHSMINISTERIUM FÜR VOLKS-AUFKLÄRUNG UND PROPAGANDA.

'Entartete' Kunst: typescript inventory. [1942?]. 2 v. Pressmark: Safe 2

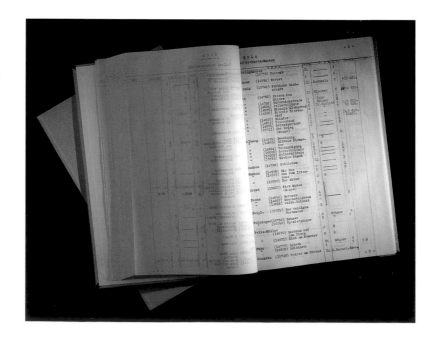

Krazy Kat

EDUARDO
PAOLOZZI (*b*.1924)

Krazy Kat Arkive of
Twentieth-Century
Popular Culture.
c. 20,000 files.
Pressmark:
AAD/1985/3;
AAD/1989/5;
AAD/1994/7;
AAD/1997/15.

'Bunk' was the title of a lecture given by
Eduardo Paolozzi to an invited audience at
the Institute of Contemporary Arts in London
in April 1952. Using an epidiascope, Paolozzi
showed images which he had created between
1947 and 1952. The images were hand-torn,
creased and stuck to papers and boards in various colours. Paolozzi's pictorial source was
that of 'science fiction, sex, technology, the
movies, mass advertising, comics, packaging'.

Sir Eduardo Paolozzi was born in Leith,
Scotland, of Italian parents. He studied art at
the Edinburgh College of Art in 1943 and at
the Slade School of Fine Art in London, from
1944 to 1947, concentrating on sculpture. He
worked in Paris from 1948 to 1950 where he
met Arp, Giacometti, Dubuffet and Tristan
Tzara, and in 1952 he was one of the founder
members of the Independent Group. As an
exponent of Pop Art, his work mirrors contemporary consumer culture, particularly the
influence of American culture on British society since the Second World War. Paolozzi's
sculptures often combine anatomical, mechanical and totemic features. His sculptures and
graphic design work are exhibited and displayed throughout the world; in London he is
perhaps best known for the mosaic wall in the
Tottenham Court Road Underground Station
and the statue of Isaac Newton for the piazza
of the new British Library.

The 'Krazy Kat Arkive of Twentieth-
Century Popular Culture' (the name is taken
from a George Herriman cartoon of the
1920s) consists of several thousand items collected by Paolozzi since the 1930s; it grew
more rapidly when he was in Paris and started
to collect images of popular culture taken
from American magazines which he obtained
from the wives of American servicemen who
were stationed there. The dominant theme of
the collection is the image of man and his
environment in the machine age, the material
also documents how dreams and values have
changed throughout the century. Many of the
images have been used as reference material
for Paolozzi's own artwork, some of which is
included within the collection.

Twiggy in Bibaland

BIBA

Fashion Retailer and
Department Store,
Records.
c. 1970–1994.
c. 500 files.
Pressmark:
AAD/1996/6

Justin de Villeneuve's sultry image of Twiggy reclining on a sofa in the peach bar at the end of the Rainbow Room sums up the world of Biba. Dressed in a 'long jersey tube of jet set with sequins, matching mittens, skull cap, Art Deco-style necklace, magenta seamed tights and suede platform court shoes', all specially designed for the photo shoot, Twiggy sends out signals of languid elegance.

Biba was founded in 1963 by Barbara Hulanicki and her husband Stephen Fitz-Simon. Hulanicki trained as a fashion illustrator at Brighton School of Art. Unable to buy the type of clothes she wanted, she began to design a range of cheap clothes, selling them by mail order. The success of her mail-order designs encouraged Hulanicki to open a boutique with her husband, selling women's clothes and accessories, and in 1964 Biba was opened in Abingdon Road, Kensington. Hulanicki's objective was to bring cheap high fashion to the masses. The merchandise reflected her personal taste for dark colours and slinky materials, especially purples and satins. The black and gold Biba logo designed by John MacConnell gave Biba goods instant recognition and appeal.

Biba's success was so considerable that in 1969, after several moves, the Biba organisation took over the Art Deco department store in Kensington High Street formerly occupied by Derry & Toms. Hulanicki employed a number of people to design and refurbish the store, including architects and shop fitters, art directors and specialists from the film industry. Steve Thomas, a founder member of the design group Whitmore-Thomas Associates, had worked for Hulanicki from 1968. In 1971 he was given the job of producing designs for all seven floors of the store, all the shop fittings such as cash tills, counters and telephone booths and the store's graphic designs and packaging. The store, which was opened in 1973, combined Art Deco and Art Nouveau styles. Ranges of merchandise on sale included cosmetics, childrenswear and menswear, food and household products. Biba ceased trading in 1975.

5 Children's Books

The National Art Library includes over 8,000 children's books of all periods, as a genre that documents the history of publishing and the art of the book. It has a number of important collections, among them the extensive library of Guy Little, acquired in 1961, and 100 books which had belonged to members of the Royal Family, presented by Queen Mary in 1936. A major collection of Beatrix Potter materials, bequeathed by Leslie Linder in 1973, attracted further acquisitions, which make the V&A's collections of Potter material the largest in the world. The NAL is also an important repository of twentieth-century Russian book production. In 1981 it acquired the Horton Collection of Soviet children's books, which accounts for two-thirds of the NAL's 300 Russian juveniles, and is a valuable adjunct to the Larionov Collection. The V&A's Prints, Drawings and Paintings Collection contains examples of related artwork.

Inevitably, this chapter omits many outstandingly original and pioneering productions, and can provide only a taste of the NAL's riches in this area. *The Butterfly's Ball* (1807), first fantasy of the nineteenth century; its successor, Edward Lear's *Book of Nonsense* (1846); the great trio, Walter Crane, Randolph Caldecott, Kate Greenaway; and from the twentieth century, Edmund Dulac, Edward Ardizzone and Maurice Sendak: all are fully represented in the collections, but not here.

The status of the children's book has often been ambiguous. The earliest items included here are educational and devotional. The religious message of the 'Hieroglyphic Bible' made such productions approved reading at a time when few entertaining picture books were available, apart from that other multi-purpose work, *Aesop's Fables*. *Aesop* was among the first books to be printed, and the first to be illustrated. Fairy tales, like fables, evolved only gradually as children's literature. There were didactic versions, some used in schools, the more vulgar and exciting chapbook versions from the pedlar's pack, and 'polite' editions, enjoyed by children despite their sophistication.

In spite of his pre-Christian and worldly wisdom, *Aesop* contrived to escape the disapproval encountered by fairy tales. Perrault's *Histoires*, one of the few texts from a European oral tradition to have survived almost unchanged to the present day, was still presented as a token lesson book in the edition of 1737 discussed here. Except for *The Arabian Nights*, which first reached the West in 1704, Perrault had no worthy successor until the Brothers Grimm.

Well represented in the collections are the enterprising eighteenth-century publisher John Newbery and his associates, who began to disseminate fairy tales and nursery rhymes. Individual tales, like rhymes, provided a lucrative source of material for both chapbook sellers and nursery anthologists. Most popular of all was 'Cinderella', one of several fairy tales with a long pantomime history; the example included here, a 'harlequinade', belongs to a genre intimately connected with the theatre, and again not intended exclusively for children.

By the late eighteenth century, both fairy tales and children had come into fashion, and colour had come to children's books. In the collections are little books from around 1800, enticingly hand-coloured, and larger-format books from the second half of the century, such as the characteristic 'toy books', crudely or lavishly colour-printed. Charles Bennett's use of colour in his hand-tinted *Aesop* anticipates the great illustrators of the next generation – Crane, Caldecott, Greenaway – but these three have none of his sinister undertones and scurrilous humour. Bennett, a particularly imaginative and witty toybook artist and a writer as well, is one of many children's book illustrators who began their careers as caricaturists.

Some of the best children's books were first addressed to real children: the works of Lewis Carroll and Kenneth Grahame, James Barrie and Beatrix Potter spring to mind. Similarly inspired were Kurt Schwitters, Jean de Brunhoff and Edward Ardizzone. Charles Bennett was no exception, though his *Aesop* is as much a picture book for adults as for children.

Beatrix Potter is represented here by an illustrated manuscript, dedicated to a child friend, but not published in its creator's lifetime and never in the form she had intended. Potter admired Randolph Caldecott with a 'jealous appreciation', and he is her most obvious influence in 'The Sly Old Cat': a perfect match of picture and text. *The Tale of Peter Rabbit* (1902) had been one of the first books printed by the trichromatic process, a technique admirably suited to the art of Arthur Rackham.

Rackham and Potter share a close, positively Pre-Raphaelite observation of the natural world; both artists needed the imaginative stimulus of 'reality'. Potter could perhaps have made her reputation entirely as a serious scientific illustrator, but in the public mind she is inextricably connected with rabbits. Similarly, Rackham might have preferred to specialise as a painter of portraits, especially portraits in a landscape, but *Peter Pan in Kensington Gardens*, and the prevailing fashion for fairies, drew him irrevocably in another direction. The gift-book layout is sometimes criticised as being 'unbookish', over-splendid and sophisticated, and 'too good for children'. Not all Rackham's work was in this format, however; he was by inclination a draughtsman, and understood the demands of the page as well as he fed the childish imagination.

A very different sensitivity to graphic composition could be found in Continental Europe. Kurt Schwitters, like Potter, was concerned to express the relationship between printed page and textual flow. His approach, however, was experimental, typography-based, and unconstrained by convention. For Russian avant-garde artists, as for Schwitters, illustration was not a lesser art, and children's books were held in high estimation. Maxim Gorky asserted that only the best is good enough for the men and women of tomorrow. Children's books are important in the development of taste and imagination. The illustrator's role is a particularly responsible one, since his images remain in the memory for life.

Children's books blossomed after the Revolution, and the USSR was the first country to introduce state control of book production, with a policy of employing foremost graphic artists. The results were astoundingly successful, considering the low level of literacy at that time. The influence of these mass-produced Soviet children's books was tremendous, especially in France. Many of the outstanding French lithographed picture books of the 1930s should be styled 'franco-russes', in particular the 90 *Albums du Père Castor*, over half of which were the work of *émigré* Russians. Links between Russian and French writers and artists had always been close. The father of Jean de Brunhoff, creator of 'Babar', had for instance produced superb programmes for Diaghilev's Ballets Russes.

Maurice Sendak wrote in 1988: 'The interplay between few words and many pictures commonly called the picture book makes aesthetic demands that few have mastered. ... Babar is at the very heart of my conception of what turns a picture book into a work of art.' Thanks to the comparative cheapness of lithography, children's books of the 1930s and 1940s are characterised by a generous size and the dominance of colour. Influences from Continental Europe began to affect British book design and illustration in the 1930s, and were transmitted to America by both Russian and German artists fleeing persecution. Soviet children's writers hid a serious message beneath a cheerful exterior. The sagas of Babar are a modern blend of fun with implicit moral instruction; their hero has become as much of an icon as Alice and Peter Pan.

Children's book illustration has been in existence for barely 250 years. A few examples stand out as original, eccentric and inspired, but the mainstream developed in tandem with the publishing establishment as a whole. Their illustrators, especially the caricaturists among them, are well represented in magazines as well as books, and can be found in the NAL's other collections. Many artists and writers found a comfortable niche in the juvenile market, perhaps from necessity, as in Soviet Russia. In recent years, picture books have been the only outlet for some talented graphic artists.

The illustrator takes the text as his guide, whether the words are those of others or his own. All the artists represented here, anonymous, neglected or celebrated, understood the immediacy of the visual, and their work in turn draws the reader in.

Abcies and Abecedaries

*TABULÆ
ABCDARIÆ
PUERILES*

[Leipzig: V. Bapst,
c. 1544].
1 fol. (printed surface
218 x 157mm)
Accession no.:
L.1955–1939
Pressmark: R.C.V.29

This rare broadsheet, one of the oldest surviving printed alphabets, is the earliest 'children's book' in the National Art Library. Its creator, Petrus Plateanus, was Rector of the Humanist Gymnasium of Zwickau, Saxony, from 1535 to 1546. His successor said of it: 'nothing could be more convenient'; a larger version served the whole school, and each pupil also had one like this, probably corresponding to the '623 A.B.C. Buchleinn' printed by Valentin Bapst. The 1545 edition of Bapst's Lutheran hymns has the same woodcut borders, made up of several pieces and thought to be the work of a specialist border cutter. These incorporate Renaissance motifs, principally acanthus-leaf ornament. Three alphabets are set in Roman and Gothic type, with lists of vowels, diphthongs and consonants, and a *Syllabarium*. Perversely, the Latin Lord's Prayer is presented in Gothic characters. The impression is crisp and of the highest quality.

The successor to such 'abecedaries' was the more versatile hornbook. Sheets of printed ABCs, each normally preceded by a cross, with the usual lists and often the Lord's Prayer, were cut up and mounted on small bats of wood or leather which could be fastened to a child's belt. Some were even edible, being made of gingerbread. The relatively indestructible hornbook could be used for playing shuttlecock: hence its flimsier and more enticing successor was called the battledore. The NAL has three eighteenth-century hornbooks, and five battledores from around 1800. Three are hand-coloured, four are backed with gilt and flowered 'Dutch' paper, and all are illustrated.

Alphabets were at first incorporated into 'primers', originally religious manuals. The earliest English abecedary (*c.*1538) is primarily a devotional book which includes an ABC. A phonetic reader by John Hart contains what may be the first English picture alphabet (1570). Its arrangement of little compartmented woodcuts with captions influenced many later layouts, among them the first pictorial encyclopaedia for children, Comenius's multilingual *Orbis pictus* (1657). The NAL has later editions of Comenius, and some eighteenth-century descendants of these early alphabets.

By 1700, ABC books began to include rhymes; by 1800, they openly aimed to entertain, often through a particular theme. Every type of alphabet, from little crude chapbooks to large cheerful picture books, is represented in the collections.

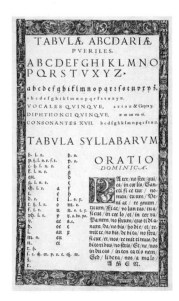

'A Diversion for Virtue-Loving Youth'

The rebus, a form of picture puzzle, seems first to have been used by Giovambattista Palatino in his treatise on penmanship of 1540. In 1684, Melchior Mattsperger, former mayor and merchant of Augsburg, devised the first 'hieroglyphic Bible', in which biblical stories were told through rebuses, as 'a diversion for virtue-loving youth'. The earliest editions survive only in single copies. Their rarity is hardly surprising, since Mattsperger encouraged readers to insert individual pictures as markers in their Bibles.

Hanns Georg Bodenehr, one of a well-known family of Augsburg artists, engraved the 84 copper plates. The title page is arranged in the shape of a heart, surrounded by emblems also within hearts. Most pages have three designs (four on f. 20), embellished with calligraphic scrollwork. Much of the original binding, adorned with floral sprays painted on vellum, has survived.

A long introductory poem is followed by three indices; one identifies the obscurer flowers which wreath the ubiquitous heart motifs, inviting the reader to colour them in. (Some early copies were issued with the figures already coloured.) Next, the passages, taken from Martin Luther's Bible, are given in full, in case the reader has no Bible to hand. After many laudatory poems by well-wishers come the *Figur-Sprüche*. At the foot of each, to be learned by heart, is a lively rhyming couplet which comments on the passage or gives its essence.

According to Mattsperger's preface for Part II (1692), Part I elicited hostile criticism, but it inspired many Continental imitations. Part II was the chief model for the first English example, *A Curious Hieroglyphic Bible* (*c.*1780), with woodcuts often attributed to Thomas Bewick. Another version, *A New Hieroglyphical Bible* (1794), was much imitated, and like most English versions, rather tediously added every text in full; the NAL has several examples.

The conceit was adopted for more light-hearted productions, such as Benjamin Franklin's *The Art of Making Money Plenty* (1817). Catherine Sinclair, author of *Holiday House* (1839), had great success with her six 'hieroglyphic stories' or letters (1861–64); *Picture Letters III* and *IV* are in the Guy Little Bequest. Riddles and puzzles are still occasionally set in rebus form.

GEISTLICHE HERZENS-EINBILDUNGEN INN ZWEIHUNDERT UND FÜNFZIG BIBLISCHEN FIGUR-SPRÜCHEN ANGEDEUTET … VON M. MATTSPERGER [Spiritual Imaginings of the Heart in 250 Illustrated Quotations from the Bible].

[Part I, 1 ed. (1684), 2nd impression.] Augstburg: H. C. Bodenehr 1685. Accession date: 24.2.1868 Pressmark: 60.Z.224

Hohelied Sal: II. v. 2.
Ich bin wie eine
im thal.
Eine
unter den

Frommes Hertz ist manches mahl,
Wie ein Roß' im Dornenthal.
84.

Hohelied Sal: V. v. 1.
Mein Freünd kome inn Seinen
und Esse Seiner Edlen

Mein Freünd kom in seine Garten,
Eß die Edle Früchtens Arten.
85.   XXVIII.

Hohel: Salom: II. v. 5.
Er erqvicket mich mit
und labet mich mit
Dann Ich bin kranck vor liebe

Jesus Liebe kan begaben,
Mehr als Blum' und Apfel Laben.
85.

Syr. XIX. v. 12.
Wenn ein Wort im
stecket, So ists eben,
als wenn ein
im der Hüfft stecket.

Eines Narren Wort und Strauß,
wie ein Pfeil im Leib muß rauß.
156.   24.

Baruch. VI. v. 21.
Die Nacht
und andere
Sizen auf ihrer Gözen
desgleichen auch die

Thiere ehren nicht die Gözen,
Weniger dan wir Sie schäzen.
155.   LII.

Esay. VI. v. 10.
Dise leüte sehen nicht mit ihren
noch hören mit Ihren
noch verstehen mit Ihrem
en
Bekehren Sich nicht:
und genesen nicht.

Sollen Sinn' und Herz genesen.
Müs bekehrung sein ihr wesen.
157.

MOTHER GOOSE's TALES

CHARLES
PERRAULT
(1628–1703)

*Histories, or Tales
of Passed Times.
With Morals.*
Written in French by
M. Perrault, and
Englished by R.S.
Gent [i.e. Robert
Samber]. 2nd ed.,
corr. London: printed
for R. Montagu and
J. Pote at Eton, 1737.
363p., [1] leaf of
plates, ill.
Accession no.:
L.6044-1961 (Guy
Little Bequest)
Pressmark: Safe 2.C.1

Mother Goose's Tales

Charles Perrault, retired civil servant and Member of the Académie Française, made the first collection of fairy tales for the young. These tales, drawn from an oral tradition, were written in plain language and are now accepted as the definitive version. Both the dedication manuscript of 1695, with five tales and illustrated in colour, and the first edition (1697), were addressed to 'Mademoiselle', niece of Louis XIV, and registered under the name of Pierre Darmancour, Perrault's son.

Robert Samber, an obscure but productive translator, took his text from the corrected Amsterdam edition of 1721, the first to recognise Perrault's authorship. The first literary English translation, on which all others were based until the early nineteenth century, it was advertised in the *Monthly Chronicle* in 1729 as 'very entertaining and instructive for children'. It starts with 'Little Red Riding Hood', first recorded by Perrault in 1695, and also includes 'L'Adroite Princesse', by Perrault's niece, Mademoiselle L'Héritier. Perrault's 'La Belle au bois dormant', first of eight tales in the 1697 collection, becomes 'The Sleeping Beauty', since Samber confused 'dormant' for 'dormante'.

This is the earliest copy extant in Britain. In the engraved frontispiece a placard bears the title 'MOTHER GOOSE'S TALES' (in French, 'CONTES DE MA MERE LOYE'), the first appearance in print of a centuries-old figure later chiefly associated with nursery rhymes. As in the original manuscript, three fashionably clothed children stand spellbound as she spins her stories and her thread. The same fireside scene with dame and cat is repeated in the first few editions; later the lettering vanishes. Without the background but with updated dress, it reappears (*c.*1820) as an elegant title page vignette (Dyce Collection 12mo 7333).

Fairy tales, considered unsuitable for children, persisted 'underground' in chapbooks. The courtly *contes* of the Comtesse d'Aulnoy appeared in English long before Perrault but less successfully. The NAL has editions both of Madame d'Aulnoy and the encyclopaedic 41-volume *Cabinet des fées* (1785–89), final monument to the vogue for literary fairy tales, an adult preserve. Not until 1772 was Perrault issued simply for the child's delight, rather than as a language manual, and he has never gone out of fashion.

Cinderella as Harlequinade

In the collection are two uncoloured examples of a popular but short-lived genre, as much a paper toy as a book: the 'harlequinade' or 'metamorphosis.' This fragile precursor of the modern 'pop-up' book is more accurately described as a 'flap picture book' or 'turn-up'. It consisted of two attached leaves. The lower sheet, printed from a single engraved plate, was folded vertically into four. The upper sheet, similarly engraved, was cut along the middle and hinged to its top and bottom edges. The resulting flaps, four above and four below, could be turned up or down to transform the picture, so telling a story which was usually presented also in a set of rather banal six-line stanzas. The whole was bound in paper wrappers.

Its ancestor seems to have been a moral work in woodcuts, *The Beginning, Progress and End of Man* (1650). The fashion was apparently started by Robert Sayer, a map and printseller who published about 15 turn-ups between 1766 and 1772 at 6d plain and 1/- coloured. Sayer, promptly imitated by other booksellers, was inspired to take his subjects from pantomimes ('harlequinades') seen at the leading London theatres. This enhanced their attraction, and their success spread to North America.

'Cinderella' is the most widespread of all fairy tales. Perrault's version, worldly rather than improving, overshadows all others, in every guise. The NAL's other harlequinade, also published by Thompson in 1804, is *Valantine* [sic] *and Orson*. A long-lived heroic legend first published in 1505, it became a favourite chapbook title and, in 1870, a Walter Crane toy book.

By the 1800s, the genre was more obviously aimed at children, and included ballads such as 'The Babes in the Wood'. From eighteenth-century pantomime, harlequinades moved into nineteenth-century melodrama, but were outmoded by the birth of the 'juvenile drama', sheets of characters and scenes with which children could make their own toy theatres. The form survives, however, in 'heads, bodies and legs' books. Manuscript precedents of both types go back at least to the seventeenth century, and persist in home-made examples up to the present day.

CINDERILLA [SIC]; *OR, THE LITTLE GLASS SLIPPER*

London: G. Thompson, 1804. 4p., ill.
Accession no.: L.462-1883
Pressmark: 60.Z.497(g)

The clock is near to twelve absorb'd in joy,
Her godmother's injunction she forgets
Poor thing I pity her neglect.
Turn down some future Ills doth her beset.

The clock has struck, O, sad reverse of fate,
She in her fright her slipper left behind,
Chang'd from her splendor, to her cindry dress,
The Prince the lost slipper he doth find.

THE DOG IN THE MANGER.

Aesop's Fables

Aesop's Fables was revived in the later nineteenth century through the inventiveness of interpreters such as C.H. Bennett. Abandoning the traditional motifs and stereotype animal characters, Bennett applied the fables to his own time. The protagonists are men in animal masks, a device used from the medieval satirists to Edward Lear, and most brilliantly by J.I. Grandville. Bennett's barbed and worldly fables, satirical portraits in elegant settings, concentrate on human follies. In *The Sad History of Greedy Jem* (1858), his characters actually turn into beasts symbolic of their vices.

Little is known of Charles Bennett's life, but he was a noted caricaturist. His first work is found in *The Puppet-Show*, an obscure magazine of the late 1840s. Some of his best creations, packed with lively wit and social comment, and detail that delights both child and adult, were inspired by his own children. Many also appeared in hand-coloured editions; examples of most are in the NAL collections. *Shadows* came out in 1857, and four remarkable and influential picture books in 1858, diverse in both technique and style. Particularly successful was the fluent narrative of his nursery rhyme ballad *The Frog Who Would a Wooing Go*, one of *Routledge's New Toy Books*, treated quite differently by Randolph Caldecott in 1880. Bennett's premature death in 1867, at the age of 38, was mourned by many distinguished men including Charles Kingsley, John Everett Millais and John Tenniel.

The *Aesop* blocks were engraved by Joseph Swain, like Bennett a *Punch* illustrator, and much involved with juvenile books. Bennett often cut his own blocks; taught how to prepare plates by George Cruikshank, he was one of the few artists at this period to use both etching and wood-engraving. The cover and frontispiece, showing a dejected young man (himself?) before a court of animals, may have served as a model for the trial scene, one of Tenniel's illustrations for *Alice in Wonderland*. In the title-page vignette the same man, grown old, looks into a mirror and sees a fox.

Charles Bennett, though one of the best Victorian comic artists, is today unjustly neglected, and his once-popular fable book comparatively little-known, although a selection was published by Gallimard in 1979.

'The Sly Old Cat'

'The Sly Old Cat', third of a trio of 'concertina' books for very young children, remained unpublished during Beatrix Potter's lifetime, and has never been issued in the original format. Known as 'Nellie's little rat story' because it was presented to the younger daughter of Harold Warne, head of Frederick Warne (the publishers), it was specially bound in blue cloth with a silver clasp. The vignettes appear on alternate pages facing the text, Potter as usual indicating her desired layout. Since the illustrations were never prepared for publication, the colour is unfinished and still subservient to the line. The narrative flow is especially reminiscent of a picture book by Randolph Caldecott. The tale is told mainly through conversation, in words of one syllable used with economy and deceptive simplicity. The Cat invites the Rat to tea, intending to eat her guest for dessert, but greed is her downfall and the Rat triumphs. Potter's pictures easily divert the eye, but this far-from-bland text would be completely satisfying even without illustrations.

Two other panoramic books were published for Christmas 1906: *The Story of a Fierce Bad Rabbit*, dedicated to Nellie's older sister Louie, and its companion, *The Story of Miss Moppet*. *The Sly Old Cat*, though planned for 1907, was cancelled, because shopkeepers were wary of such fragile productions, easily damaged by customers.

Nineteen of Beatrix Potter's 23 'Little Books' span a brief period between *The Tale of Peter Rabbit* (1902) and her marriage in 1913. By 1916, Warne had converted both published panoramas to the standard format and now planned to publish 'The Sly Old Cat'. Its title appears in an endpaper from November 1916, but a year later it had disappeared. Potter did not relish the idea of redrawing the pictures. She suggested commissioning Ernest Aris as illustrator: 'His plagiarisms are unblushing, and his drawing excellent'.

The manuscript was returned to Warne, and is now one of several literary manuscripts in the Linder Bequest. Leslie Linder included 'The Sly Old Cat' in *A History of the Writings of Beatrix Potter* (1971), and persuaded Warne to print it at last in conventional book form, as a twenty-fourth 'Tale'.

BEATRIX POTTER
(1866–1943)

'The Sly Old Cat'.
Folding panorama.
20 March 1906.
Pressmark:
Linder Bequest
LB 1275 (BP.597)

Peter Pan in Kensington Gardens

SIR JAMES
MATTHEW
BARRIE
(1860–1937)

*Peter Pan in
Kensington Gardens*.
With drawings by
Arthur Rackham
(1867–1939).
London: Hodder and
Stoughton 1906.
125p., 50 leaves of
plates, col. ill.
Accession no.:
L.3941-1980
Pressmark: 60.BB.288

Peter Pan in Kensington Gardens, the Christmas gift book for 1906, first established Arthur Rackham as an artist of the fantastic. J.M. Barrie extracted its text from his 'whimsical, sentimental' *Little White Bird*, which predated the famous play by two years. The collaboration between Rackham and Barrie was initiated by Messrs Ernest Brown and Phillips of the Leicester Galleries, who in 1905 had exhibited Rackham's illustrations for *Rip Van Winkle*.

Peter Pan's popularity may be gauged from its complicated publishing history. The edition was limited to 500 vellum-bound copies; 50 plates, printed on glossy 'art paper' and half-mounted on thick brown paper with tissue-guards, follow the text. After the cloth-bound trade edition, French and American editions, and 'small' trade edition, came a 'preposterously expensive' *Peter Pan Portfolio* (1912) consisting of 12 much-enlarged plates. The cheapened *Peter Pan Retold for Little People* (1929) spoiled the original proportions: Rackham altered the imprint in one copy to 'Hangmen: drawing and quartering a speciality'. Together with *Rip Van Winkle*, *Peter Pan* made Rackham's reputation.

Modern editions do scant justice to the subtle tints, set off by a muted raw umber wash laid over the pen line. *Peter Pan* revealed Rackham's range and his mastery of composition. It introduced many characteristics of his work: the idyllic, the humorous and the grotesque; the 'Rackham tree'; sensitivity to landscape and a 'sense of place'. Above all, there were the fairies, for which his public clamoured. Rackham's fairies are a part of nature, involved with humans only unwillingly. There is an uneasy tension between Edwardian respectability and a hidden life among the tree-roots.

Rackham's mannerisms became clichés only in the hands of his imitators. Success in exhibition abroad kept pace with continuing success in publishing: *Alice in Wonderland* (1907), *A Midsummer Night's Dream* (1908) and the two-volume visualisation of Wagner's *Ring* (1910–11). Such lavish productions, destined for the drawing room rather than the nursery, did not survive long in the post-war world, but Rackham adapted his style and his format to changing circumstances, losing neither reputation nor employment. His last book, *The Wind in the Willows* (1940), was a longed-for commission, deferred from nearly 30 years before. It was completed on his death-bed.

Fairy Tales for Our Time

The *Märchen unserer Zeit*, created by Kurt Schwitters in collaboration with Käthe Steinitz, were intended to be 'fairy tales for our time', radical yet timeless. The designer Theo van Doesburg, who was Steinitz's husband, suggested making a picture book using nothing but typographical elements. The result was *Die Scheuche* (The Scarecrow), planned *en famille*, in improvisatory mood: Schwitters declaimed his new poem while van Doesburg laid out matches on the kitchen table, arranging them in the shape of a scarecrow. Elements from the type-case were chosen for emotional expressiveness: a diagonal 'b' for feet, and a sharply angled 'B' for the angry farmer's body. The typesetter, Paul Vogt, entered into the spirit, cutting an especially large 'O' for Monsieur le Coq.

Schwitters had joined the Dada Movement in 1918, but was ostracised by the Berlin Dada extremists for his apolitical approach: 'I prefer nonsense, but that's a purely personal matter!' He valued wit and humour in art, and wrote other, more satirical fairy tales. Schwitters took issues of design and typography as seriously as painting, making no significant distinction between fine and applied arts. In 1919 he established 'MERZ', his own form of Dada. 'Merz', a word fragment taken from a scrap of newspaper, used a random collection of waste objects, in constructions and collages. *Der Hahnepeter, Die Scheuche* and *Die Märchen vom Paradies* were originally published in 1924–25 as numbers of the periodical *Merz*.

Influenced by Constructivism, and interested in the appearance of words as well as their meaning, Schwitters had in 1923 turned his attention to typography and advertising. 'Aposs' replaced 'MERZ' as Schwitters's imprint, specialising in the publication of children's books. 'APOSS', his new motto, stood for 'aktiv, paradox, ohne Sentimentalität, sensibel'. 'Our great project was more bold than profitable', wrote Steinitz. Never commercially published, the *Märchen* went virtually unnoticed, and in any case Schwitters had suddenly turned to architecture.

In early twentieth-century Germany, the power of oral tradition was still taken seriously, and all progressive experiments with folklore were banned by the Nazis. Regarded as decadent, Schwitters emigrated to Norway in 1937, fleeing to England in 1940. He received almost no public recognition in his lifetime, but is now considered one of the great pioneers of twentieth-century art.

KURT SCHWITTERS (1887–1948), KÄTHE (KATE) STEINITZ (*d.*1975) AND THEO VAN DOESBURG (1883–1931)

Die Scheuche Märchen [The scarecrow's tale]. Hannover: Apossverlag 1925. [12] p., ill.
Accession no.: L.1827-1937
Pressmark: 95.JJ.96

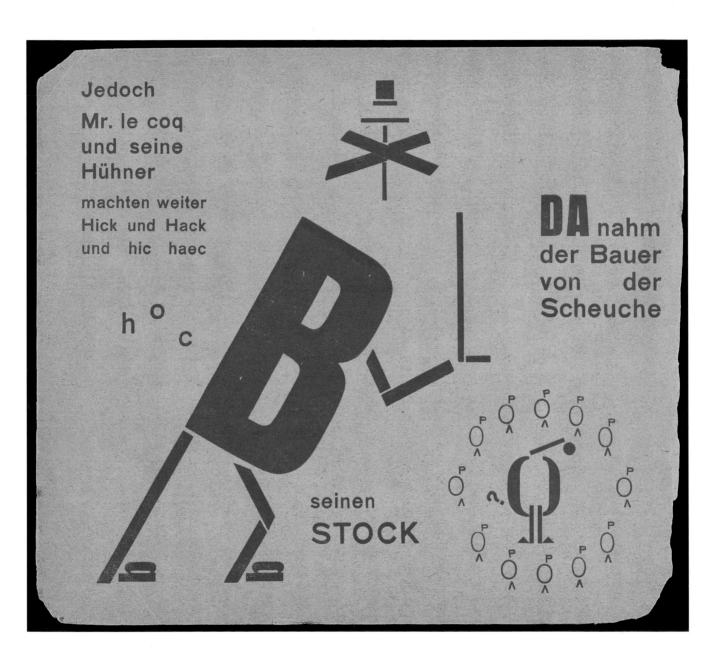

Побежала мышка-мать
Стала свинку в няньки звать:
—Приходи к нам, тетя свинка,
Нашу детку покачать.

Стала нянька хрипло хрюкать,
Стала глупого баюкать:

—Баю-баюшки, хрю-хрю,
Я морковку подарю.

Глупый маленький мышонок
Отвечает ей спросонок:
—Нет, твой голос не хорош,—
Очень грубо ты поешь.

Побежала мышка-мать
Тетю лошадь в няньки звать:
—Приходи к нам, тетя лошадь,
Нашу детку покачать.

—И-го-го!—поет лошадка.—
Спи, мышонок, сладко-сладко,
Повернись на правый бок,
Дам овса тебе мешок.

Глупый маленький мышонок
Отвечает ей спросонок:
—Нет, твой голос не хорош,—
Очень страшно ты поешь.

A Foolish Little Mouse

SAMYL
IAKOVLEVICH
MARSHAK
(1887–1964)

*O glupom myshonke
[About a Foolish Little
Mouse].* Illustrated by
Vladimir Vasil'evich
Lebedev (1891–1967).
7 edn. Leningrad:
Detgiz 1935. [6]
leaves, col. ill.
Accession date:
20.v.1936
Pressmark: 36 BB.23

'Every book for children should be colourful, out of the ordinary, striking to the eye' (V.V. Lebedev). After the Revolution, children's books in the USSR became a laboratory for artistic experiment. Visually arresting, and printed in vast paperback editions, few copies survive. Texts tended to be short, and design of typography, cover and illustrations integrated. The compositions, usually in bold chalk without drawn outlines, are vivid and full of movement. Soviet children's books amazed those who saw them in Paris and Berlin in the 1920s: daring in style, of high quality, yet cheap.

V.V. Lebedev was one of the few Soviet illustrators who did not emigrate, in spite of oppression. Famous for his 'agit-prop' posters for the Russian Telegraph Agency (ROSTA), he used the same arresting language for his early, collage-based children's books, notably *Tsirk* (*Circus*). These geometric abstract designs, evidence of descent from the *lubok* or Russian popular print, later become more plastic and pictorial, especially after the Second World War, when animal subjects predominate in his work. In this cautionary tale, first published in 1925, the little mouse dislikes the voices of his mother and of other animal nurses, but lets himself be charmed by the cat. At the end, the mouse mother finds an empty bed: children's eyes must be opened to the reality as well as to the beauty of the world. The 1953 edition has new pictures, less 'artistic' but more touching.

With Samyl Marshak, Lebedev headed the Children's Section (Leningrad Region) of the State Publishing House. Founded in 1925, it reflected the most innovative features of contemporary art, and assembled the best artists and writers. Marshak created a special new literature in verse for the 'pre-school child', from three to seven, and Lebedev's early books influenced most of his contemporaries and successors. In 1933 the Children's Section was subordinated to Detgiz (Detizdat), the Moscow-based 'State Editions for Children'. Social Realism, born after the First Congress of Soviet Writers (1934), stifled the creative freedom of Lebedev and his pupils. *Émigré* disciples of Lebedev created many of the best French lithographed children's books of the 1930s, especially the Père Castor albums; and so, indirectly, our own *Puffin Picture Books* descend from Lebedev.

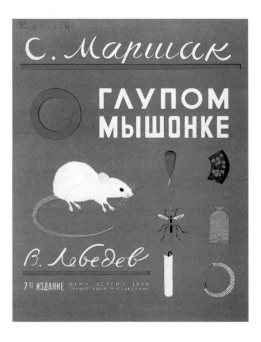

Babar the Elephant

'Voilà la mer, la grande mer bleue.' The allure of Babar comes partly from the grandeur of Jean de Brunhoff's double-page spreads, and partly from its hero, that most intelligent yet sympathetically human elephant. The airy compositions have something of Raoul Dufy, whom de Brunhoff much admired; the warm but unsentimental domestic scenes recall Carl Larssen. Maurice Sendak, for whom the artist's skill in depicting both distance and detail evoke the panoramas of van Eyck, adds: 'The grace and graphic charm are almost sufficient by themselves, but to deny the message is to deny the full weight of Jean de Brunhoff's genius.'

Urbanity overlies a profound ideal of civilised public life and dedication to the family. Each story is a miniature Homeric epic; the hero overcomes misfortune and evil through courage and perseverance. There is a seemingly effortless selective shorthand of both word and line, in which everything, commonplace or extraordinary, has its place: even death, which comes so shockingly at the start of the first book, *L'histoire de Babar* (1931).

Le voyage de Babar (1932) was the second of seven picture books created between 1931 and 1937, the year of Jean de Brunhoff's untimely death from tuberculosis. Instantly popular, Babar soon travelled to England and America. Methuen brought out *The Story of Babar* in 1933 with a preface by A.A. Milne, and *Babar's Travels* in 1935. The early books were reproduced, in full size, directly from the artwork; by 1933 de Brunhoff had changed his method, to hand-colouring the proofs. His brother-in-law was a director of Jardin des Modes, and his brother Michel its chief editor, and publisher of *Vogue*. An awareness of this world of taste and fashion is evident in the books.

In 1946, de Brunhoff's oldest son Laurent, who had often advised his father on colours, revived the national hero 'Babar', in what he called 'faithfulness to the father style'. Over 30 titles followed. The son's facility lacks the subtle delicacy of his father's work. More damaging was the reduction in scale forced by high production costs. Some of the early stories have now been reissued in the original format, so that children can once more 'climb into' a Babar book.

JEAN DE
BRUNHOFF
(1899–1937)

Le voyage de Babar.
Paris: Éditions du
Jardin des Modes,
Groupe des
Publications Condé
Nast 1932.
47p., col. ill.
Accession no.:
L.1406-1935
Pressmark:
60.AA.211

Le pays des éléphants est loin maintenant.
Sans bruit le ballon glisse dans le ciel.
Babar et Céleste regardent le paysage.
Quel beau voyage !
L'air est doux, le vent léger.
Voilà la mer, la grande mer bleue.

Alice in Wonderland

LEWIS CARROLL
(1832–1898)

Lewis Carroll's Through the Looking-Glass and What Alice Found There.
Illustrated by Barry Moser (*b.*1940).
West Hatfield, Mass.: Pennyroyal Press, 1982.
xix, 163 p., ill.
Accession no.: L.4324-1985
Pressmark: 95.QQ.27

A book 'ought to mean a great deal more than the writer meant', said Lewis Carroll. Perhaps this can also apply to the illustrator? Barry Moser denies that the Duchess in his 1982 *Alice's Adventures in Wonderland* was modelled on Richard Nixon. Several portraits in his *Looking-Glass* were, however, taken from life, including an intentional President Nixon, as Humpty Dumpty. The distorted, vertiginous perspective echoes the tall narrow format.

Trade editions of both *Alice* and *Looking-Glass* were published by the University of California Press in 1982 and 1983, allowing additional refinements to be made under Moser's direction. Both texts were edited by Selwyn Goodacre, with notes and a preface by the Victorian scholar James Kincaid.

'I have tried to keep the [*Alice*] illustrations weird (yet reasonable), and grotesque (yet humorous), but I have not tried to make them pretty or graceful.' Moser's *Looking-Glass* designs similarly avoid the familiar, but by restoring the Jabberwock to the frontispiece he revives the author's original intention; Carroll had removed Tenniel's frightening Jabberwock to a less prominent place, substituting the White Knight. Moser also restores the long-lost 'Wasp in a wig' episode, rejected by Carroll and discovered again in 1974, as an 'alternative reading' of Chapter VIII.

Only through a looking-glass does the reader see Alice within her dream – as she would see herself. 'Mirrored pairs' occur throughout, in preliminary and after matter and in the Queens, Knights, Tweedles, and even Lion and Unicorn. The letter-forms are seen as in a mirror, except when Alice herself writes out a mathematical problem for Humpty Dumpty. The formality of the chess game suggested to Moser a 'more exacting resolution' for the *Looking-Glass* images than for those of *Wonderland*. 'They are images of greater refinement and logic ... and ... strive for a ... more deliberate degree of finish.'

'Two graphic notions are important to me: tension and surface.' Barry Moser, one of the foremost etcher–engravers in the USA, studied with Leonard Baskin. He is proprietor of the Pennyroyal Press and director of the Hampshire Typothetae. Several of his works are in the NAL; his most recent production is *The Pennyroyal Caxton Bible* (1999). Moser's *Alice* won the American Book Award for Design-Pictorial in 1983.

Clown's Quest

Clown is a wordless picture book in which the outstanding talent and distinctive style of its author and illustrator, Quentin Blake, is perfectly demonstrated. The book is structured as a strip-cartoon, the most dynamic form of visual storytelling, giving immediacy and impact to the story-line. The lively, apparently spontaneous, line drawing adds to the pace of the narrative so that the reader is carried along with Clown and the urgency of his quest. Thrown out by his owner together with his soft-toy friends, Clown undergoes various trials and adventures before succeeding in finding them all a new home. Without dialogue, the 'reader' is stimulated both emotionally and visually, having to create a story from the pictures.

Blake's skill lies in vigorous composition and expressive line. Through *Clown* he communicates a range of emotions with the economy of a mime artist. He instils mood through scale and colour, from the grey overpowering backdrop of an impersonal city to the warm and cosy glow of a loving home.

Clown is one of several works by Quentin Blake in the collection. It received a number of awards in 1996, including the National Art Library Illustration Awards second prize for books; the Bronze Award in the 0–5 years category Nestlé Smarties Book Prize; *New York Times* Best Illustrated Book; and the Bologna Ragazzi Award.

Quentin Blake is a prize-winning author and illustrator of children's books whose illustrious career spans more than 40 years. Although he had no formal art training, he has drawn from an early age, having work published in *Punch* at the age of 16. He taught illustration at the Royal College of Art, where he was Head of Department from 1978 until 1986, and is now a visiting tutor. He has successfully collaborated with authors such as Joan Aitken, Roald Dahl, Russell Hoban, Michael Rosen and John Yeoman. He won the 1980 Kate Greenaway medal for *Mister Magnolia* and in 1999 was voted the first Children's Laureate.

QUENTIN BLAKE
(*b*.1932)

Clown.
London: [Jonathan] Cape 1995.
[32] p., col. ill.
ISBN: 0224045105
Pressmark:
60.HH.131

6 Comics

Comics are a very popular publishing format and they have influenced many generations across their entire spectrum – from reading for children to inspiration for mature artists and illustrators. Indeed, for many, comics have been their first visual aesthetic experience.

What could be called the incunabula of comics were created in Geneva by Rodolphe Töpffer between 1833 and 1845. His first book, *Histoire de Mr Jabot*, a sophisticated satire in images greatly admired by Goethe, differs from contemporary comics only for having the text written as captions under each image, instead of being inserted in balloons.

Modern comics appeared in the form of comic strips from the end of the nineteenth century. In England, *Ally Sloper's Half Holiday* took the country by storm with its slapstick humour, while in the United States comic strips were closely linked to the evolution of the Sunday newspaper pages. In 1895 Joseph Pulitzer asked the artist Richard F. Outcault to produce a comic strip for the Sunday edition of the *New York World*. The strip, called *Down Hogan's Alley*, soon became very popular and widely imitated. Between 1897 and 1932 many newspaper strips were reprinted in book form, but the first true comic book appeared only in 1933 when the Eastern Color Printing Company of Waterbury, Connecticut, reduced in size and printed two Sunday comic pages side by side on one tabloid page, which was then folded to an eleven-by-eight-inch format.

The comic-book format became extremely popular following the success of the first 'Superman' story by Jerry Siegel and Joe Shuster in the first issue of *Action Comics* in 1938. 'Superman' heralded the birth of the superhero genre in which costumed people of extraordinary or superhuman powers fought evil and crime on a grand scale. Superhero comics were aimed at children and young adults, and in the long run have proved to be the most successful of all comic genres.

The 1960s witnessed the explosion of the 'comix' phenomenon in the United States, the irreverent world of the so-called underground comics, published outside the established channels. In those days Robert Crumb, one of the gurus of contemporary comics, began his career as an alternative cartoonist, reaching notoriety in 1968 with his comic book *Zap*. The 1960s and '70s were also momentous years for superhero comics, which were rejuvenated by the appearance of *The Fantastic Four*, a new and more complex interpretation of the genre by writer/editor Stan Lee and artist Jack Kirby.

Another milestone in the history of comics was the publication in 1978 of Will Eisner's *A Contract with God*. This comic is generally acknowledged to be the first example of the graphic novel, a one-shot publication in book form with a continuous comic narrative. Graphic novels, and many other comic genres, have since progressed to become sophisticated works of graphic literature – Art Spiegelmann's *Maus*, winner of a Pulitzer Prize in 1992, and his graphic magazine *Raw*, being perhaps the best-known examples. Even the superhero genre evolved towards more mature stories with the publication of Alan Moore's seminal work *Watchmen* (1986–87).

This sophistication, alas, has yet failed to catch on with the wider public in Anglo-Saxon countries, where comics of all genres are still bundled together and branded by most as superhero juvenile trivia. This attitude is in striking contrast to the wide popularity of comics in Continental Europe. In more recent years, *2000 AD*, the all-British best-selling science-fiction comic book, has managed to gain an audience even in the United States, becoming a showcase for many British artists often later lured by the greener pastures of American comics. But that is still a far cry from the success of titles like *Tex*, a Western comic created in 1948 by G.L. Bonelli and artist A. Galleppini, which is one of the longest-running comic books in existence, and with 300,000 copies sold each month, one of the best-sellers in its native Italy.

The NAL recognises that comics are a literary and visual phenomenon which is fully part of the twentieth-century cultural experience, and comics are therefore collected as examples of book production, design, illustration, and as visual resources, cultural indicators, and examples of popular culture.

The collecting pattern for comics has varied during the life of the NAL. During the nineteenth century, illustrated books and children's books were actively collected (as they are today), and some of the classic precursors of modern comics found their way into the collections, like Töpffer's *Histoire de Mr Jabot*. The NAL's coverage of comics was very uneven until the mid-1980s, but over the past 15 years the Library has been able to make some notable additions to its holdings of comics. A major acquisition was made in 1990 when the NAL acquired the Rakoff Collection of Comics, some 17,000 items amassed by the film writer/editor Ian Rakoff. This collection provides a comprehensive tapestry of twentieth-century comics, charting the growth of the genre from the newspaper strips of the first years of this century to the New Wave comics of the 1980s, consisting predominantly of four-colour American comic books. Other comics are to be found in the Renier Collection of Children's Books, and Sir Eduardo Paolozzi's *Krazy Kat Arkive* (see p.93) includes some 4,200 comics, the great majority of which are American comic books from the 1960s and '70s.

The NAL's collection of comics continues to grow, and is international in its scope, the aim being to document the main genres and the historical trends of this major publishing phenomenon.

Histoire de Mr Jabot

Rodolphe Töpffer's *Histoire de Mr Jabot* is generally acknowledged to be the first modern comic, and is one of the masterpieces of graphic storytelling.

Mr Jabot, drawn in 1831 and published by the artist himself in Geneva in 1833, tells the story of a clumsy and vain bourgeois who tries to succeed in society by displaying dandyish attitudes. Through a series of hilarious vicissitudes he manages at the end, despite himself, to marry a marchioness: a pungent satire on social climbers.

The story runs through a series of sequentially unfolding drawings contained within panel borders, with text written below each image. Töpffer developed what he called 'visages de synthèse', i.e. the combination of certain graphic signs which allowed his cartoony characters to express feelings and moods. Static images were in this way turned into dynamic sequential stories. Töpffer was also a pioneer in managing a perfect interdependence between images and text.

Töpffer himself commented upon his graphic novels in the following terms in the *Bibliothèque universelle de Genève* (1837):

Each picture is accompanied by one or two lines of text. The pictures, without this text, would have only an obscure meaning; the text, without the pictures, would mean nothing. Together they form a sort of novel, all the more original in that it does not resemble a novel more than any other thing. If [the author] is an artist, he draws badly, but he has some skill in writing; if he is a writer, he writes only moderately well, but in recompense he has a good amateur's drawing skills.

The book is lithographed throughout by the autographic process. The artist drew the images and wrote the captions on transfer paper with a pen, and the whole was later transferred on to lithographic stone. The result is one of great immediacy and freedom of line.

Töpffer soon achieved great fame in Europe. His work was greatly admired by Goethe and influenced artists of the calibre of Cham, Gustave Doré and Wilhelm Busch.

RODOLPHE
TÖPFFER
(1799–1846)

Histoire de Mr Jabot.
Genève: [the author],
1833. 52 leaves,
chiefly ill.
Pressmark: S900260

Persuadée que c'est un Suicide en Sa faveur, la Marquise S'évanouit.

Son chien aussi.

Mr. Jabot Sauve Ses jours en changeant de linge.

Ce qui fait plaisir à Mr. Jabot c'est que Ses jambes n'ont pas Souffert le moins du monde.

Ally Sloper's Half Holiday

FOUNDED AND CONDUCTED BY GILBERT DALZIEL.
SATURDAY, MARCH 20, 1897.

Vol. XIV.—No. 673.] [ONE PENNY.

'VARSITY CREWS, BEWARE!

"*Poor dear Papa, how awfully keen he is on sport. Though barely recovered from his recent steeplechase accident, he is now hard at work coaching an eight, with which he intends to challenge the winner of the University Boatrace. Very naturally, however, he fights rather shy of horseback, and may be seen any day shouting his instructions from the saddle of a fearsome thing in bikes. Like most boating coaches, Dad's language is distinctly forcible, and I'm told that when he came to grief the other afternoon, and emerged from his impromptu header, the air in the vicinity of the towpath was positively sulphurous.*"—TOOTSIE.

ARCTIC LOGIC.

"Reg'lar rot, I call it! What's the use of calling it a Pole
it it ain't a point!"

TRUE!

She. But why isn't marriage just as risky for us as for you!
Ovnie (age 19). Because, anyway a girl can't marry a woman!

A STARK-NAKED MURDERER.

JOHN PENNY, gentleman, lived in Clement's Inn, Strand, in 1741, and kept as his servant one James Hall, who, "not having the fear of God before his eyes, did traitorously, feloniously, and wilfully, and of malice aforethought, make an assault with a certain iron bar, valued twopence, and did strike the said Penny, giving him one mortal wound which broke his skull, of which mortal wound he then and there instantly died."

He was also indicted for stealing a lancet with a tortoise-shell handle, a pair of steel scissors, a blade of a knife, a blade of a penknife, a pair of tweezers, a pair of steel spurs, a silver pencil, two razors, a pair of gloves, twelve guineas and twenty half-guineas, a green silk purse and seven sticks of sealing-wax.

He was soon suspected, arrested, tried, and pleaded guilty, and when under sentence of death made an extraordinary confession. "I had a design of murdering my master," he says, "for about a month or more before I did it, having kept pretty much company of late, and spent what I had, and being resolved to stay no longer. That night (the 18th of June) my master came home between eleven and twelve, and I pulled off his shoes and outer stockings, and he was walking to his bedside with his inner stockings on, when I came behind him with a large oak stick, which I had kept under the bed for some time for that purpose, and knocked him down at one blow, and I am very sure he

Ally Sloper's Half Holiday

ALLY SLOPER'S
HALF HOLIDAY

London: Dalziel
1884–1923.
Pressmark: PC 8/3
no.1

Ally Sloper's Half Holiday was the first weekly magazine to be based around a comic strip character. It was one of the first comics to be produced in Britain and had the greatest influence on the layouts of its contemporaries.

Ally Sloper's Half Holiday, 'being a selection, side-splitting, sentimental, and serious, for the benefit of old boys, young boys, odd boys generally, and even girls', began publication on 3 May 1884. It was created to showcase the already nationally famous title character, a ne'er-do-well in the vein of Mr Micawber, created by Charles Henry Ross and his wife Marie Duval, alias Isabelle Émilie de Tessier. Sloper made his first appearance in a strip entitled 'Some mysteries of loan and discount' in the satirical magazine *Judy* on 14 August 1867, and soon became an icon of the times. He was the first character in Britain to star in his own comic book with *Ally Sloper: a moral lesson* (1873). The success of this spawned further regularly issued reprints, such as the annual *Ally Sloper's Comic Kalendar* (1876–84) and *Ally Sloper's Summer Number* (1880–84).

From today's perspective, a weekly Sloper venture seems only logical, but *Ally Sloper's Half Holiday* was in fact the first comic to introduce a fixed order to its pages with regular features placed in the same position each week. Its style was also more unified than its predecessors, whose text and cartoon features had tended to form distinct parts of the paper. The publishers, the Dalziel brothers, initially filled the pages with strips reprinted from *Judy*, but the title's success prompted the creation of more original material. New Ally cartoons adorned the cover from no.13 onwards, composed of single panels drawn by W.G. Baxter and, later, W.F. Thomas. Another *Judy* strip, 'The McNab' by James Brown, was continued as part of the centre spread. Sales peaked at 350,000 copies a week, and publication continued until the final regular *Half Holiday* in 1923.

Tex

Tex is a very popular Italian Western comic book and the longest-running Italian comic. First published as a weekly comic strip on 30 September 1948, it started as a cottage industry in war-shattered Italy. The character of Tex Willer was created by Gianluigi Bonelli, and graphically realised by Galep (the pseudonym of Aurelio Galleppini). The publisher was Tea Bonelli (Gianluigi's ex-wife), who used the drawing room of her Milanese flat as the general office of Edizioni Audace and rented a room to Galep.

Tex is an outlaw who later becomes a Texas Ranger, Indian Agent and Chief of the Navajos under the name of Night Eagle. In his adventures he is flanked by one or more of his pards: Kit Carson (the historical figure, although romanticised), his son Kit Willer, born of his marriage to a Navajo woman called Lilyth, and Tiger Jack, a fearless Navajo warrior. Characters and stories were heavily influenced by Hollywood Western mythology. Tex fights for justice, and knows no half-measures: his stories are full of shoot-outs (so far he has killed over 150 people – all villains!) and fist-fights. He is invincible, not in the superhero sense, but because of his intelligence, stamina, amazing ability with guns and his single-minded purpose in life.

The hallmark of the comic book since its inception has been the clarity and immediacy of the drawings and a detailed, articulate and witty plot built around a solid structure. In Tex a crime is committed; Tex gets involved; the villains try to kill him; Tex captures one of the villains and makes him confess; the main villain is killed. Gianluigi Bonelli scripted every story until 1976 when his son Sergio, under the pseudonym of Guido Nolitta, began sharing the task. In 1983 Claudio Nizzi became the main scripter. Galep drew most of the comics until the mid-1960s, when other artists began to contribute regularly, among them Fernando Fusco, Guglielmo Letteri and Giovanni Ticci. Tex is still one of the best-selling Italian comics, with over 300,000 copies sold each month.

TEX GIGANTE. II SERIE.

Milano: Audace 1958-present. v., ill. [Publisher varies]. Pressmark: COP.97.0004

32

The Fantastic Four

STAN LEE (*b.*1922)
AND JACK KIRBY
(*b.*1917)

The Fantastic Four.
New York: Marvel
1961–70. v., ill.
Pressmark:
RAK.BOX.108B

'The World's Greatest Comic Book.' This was how *The Fantastic Four* billed itself, and for almost a decade during the 1960s it might well have been true. It was first published in 1961 by Marvel Comics and was produced by the formidable partnership of writer Stan Lee and artist Jack Kirby.

The Fantastic Four was successful on a number of levels. On a creative level, it ushered in a new type of superhero: the so-called 'superhero with super problems'. This humanised and often self-doubting type of superhero was a radical departure from the clear-cut morals of characters like 'Superman' (made popular two decades earlier by DC Comics). It gave Stan Lee the opportunity to explore the way normal people might react when invested with extraordinary powers. *The Fantastic Four* were a varied bunch: the intellectual leader, Read Richards; the vulnerable Invisible Girl; impetuous youth in the shape of the Human Torch; and the self-loathing behemoth, The Thing – a grotesque orange-skinned creature of immense strength. They behaved like a dysfunctional family who would bicker and argue as they saved the world, and their deeds were often far from heroic. The Thing was prone to destructive bouts of bad temper and the Human Torch had all the discipline of the average teenage rebel.

This modernised view of a super team was illustrated with power and panache by Jack Kirby. He created action-packed comics full of futuristic machinery and strange-looking villains, realised with visual fluency and elegant design. Perhaps his most memorable creations were Galactus, a cosmic deity who consumes planets as food, and the Silver Surfer, who roams the skies on a surf board (a perfect icon for '60s youth culture).

The Fantastic Four provided a blueprint for a numerous other successful titles (mostly by Stan Lee and Jack Kirby). Their combination of action, artistry, wittiness and carefully crafted characterisations opened up comics to a more mature readership and helped start a trend towards more adult-oriented comics. Few have come close to Kirby and Lee's perfect chemistry in the genre of superhero comics.

Zap Comix

Comics as a medium of personal expression took a giant leap forward in 1968 when Robert Crumb and his publisher friend Don Donahue produced the first run of *Zap* under the Apex Novelties imprint. Spawned by the hippie counter-culture of San Francisco, whose values it reflected and satirised, the artwork (created the year before) was consciously conceived outside the commercial mainstream. As such, Crumb felt free to pursue a blatantly personal, let-it-all-hang-out, self-expressive approach of a directness hitherto unseen in the history of comics.

Since the mid-1960s, work of a similar nature (including parts of *Zap #1*) had only previously appeared as isolated strips in certain American counter-culture publications such as *Yarrowstalks* and *The East Village Other*. However, in *Zap #1* it was published for the first time in the form of a single, self-contained comic book, and thus represents the historical emergence of a new genre: 'comix', the 'x' indicating an outsider status from the mainstream.

Unexpectedly, *Zap* was an immediate success and ultimately a revolutionary one. As the first widely available underground comic, it became a catalyst for a publishing boom in titles of a similar nature. Exploiting the accessibility of new smaller offset-litho printing machines, the American comix of the 1960s and '70s pioneered the concept of the small independent publisher producing niche-market, adult-oriented comics. The comic-book form was taken beyond the constraints of the dominant children's market. This important development has since been continued by creative artists and publishers interested in expanding the expressive potential of the medium.

Although Crumb relinquished editorial control after the second issue (*Zap #0*), he continued to contribute to the title when it subsequently became a compendium vehicle for leading talents in the American comix scene, sporadically published under the Print Mint imprint. Widely available as reprints, original early runs are now highly sought-after collectors' items.

Crumb continues to produce new work for small independent imprints. His output remains as personal and iconoclastic as ever, and his reputation as one of the greatest artists of the medium seems unassailable.

ZAP COMIX

San Francisco:
Apex Novelties
1968–78. v., ill.
[Publisher varies].
Pressmark:
RAK.BOX.166A

A Contract with God

WILL EISNER
(b.1917)

A Contract with God
and Other Tenement
Stories. New York:
Baronet 1978.
[191] p., ill.
ISBN 0894370359.
Pressmark:
COM.99.0004

A Contract with God is one of the first examples of a new kind of comic that became known as the 'graphic novel'. Written and drawn by Will Eisner and first published in 1978, It represents a crowning achievement in an illustrious career dating back to the 1930s.

Graphic novels generally are much longer than conventional comic books and are aimed at an adult readership. Eisner used this extended format to create four short stories set in a run-down tenement block in 1930s New York. The stories are based on Eisner's own experiences as a youth and provide an intimate account of America's newly settled Jewish community.

The stories tell of the lives, loves, triumphs and losses of the residents of 55 Dropsie Avenue. In themselves they are unremarkable; the genius lies in the way Eisner perfectly weaves together prose and images to form an entirely convincing and compelling recreation of his childhood memories.

The book is of a smallish format (similar to a paperback novel) and printed in sepia ink, which seems in keeping with the idea of an old man recounting his memoirs. The percussive rhythm of each narrative is driven by Eisner's confident (though never slick) drawing style. Only the minimum of line, shade and detail is used to describe each scene. The reader is never invited to ponder a particular drawing or sequence. Instead, each panel links seamlessly to the next to create a real sense of time and movement. This effect is enhanced by sparing use of text and carefully modulated size and style of script. The overall effect is a compelling and veritable master-class in how to use pictures and words together to create a sense of the real (something that Eisner explored more literally in his books on how to write and draw comics).

There is no 'big idea' behind A Contract with God. It consists of simple tales of city life illustrated with exceptional artistry and economy. It is in no way sensational or glamorous (two traits commonly associated with the medium of comics). What touches the reader is the human scale of its intentions. It is a remarkable and moving piece of comics storytelling.

Raw

From its inception, *Raw* was a ground-breaking graphic magazine. For the first time, someone lavished attention on the design and printing of a journal devoted to comics. If a strip was better shown printed in a particular colour, or on a particular paper, or at a particular size, the editors obliged, but the work and expense involved meant that publication was limited to twice a year.

The first issue appeared in 1980, edited, featuring and published by Art Spiegelman and his wife Françoise Mouly. He was a New Yorker and an underground/alternative comic book creator. She was French, a graphic designer, editor and artist interested in European comics. Together they brought a connoisseur's eye to publishing what is the best anthology journal of contemporary comics.

As editors, Spiegelman and Mouly attracted contributors by proposing to share any profit that might be made equally amongst them. They also guaranteed that work would be displayed to its best advantage in the company of the cream of contemporary international talent and alongside interesting examples from the history of the art form. They promoted an aficionado's sense of a Pulp aesthetic, incorporating various gimmicks from issue to issue such as bubblegum, stickers, and a hand-torn cover. *Raw* turned the spotlight on an underexposed body of idiosyncratic and fresh work dispersed across the print media. It focused attention on individuals who were often destined to careers unsuccessful in commercial terms working in the small underground market.

Raw also played an influential role in the development of the concept of the graphic novel – a form it significantly contributed to via spin-off publications called 'Raw One-Shots'. These titles were intended to feature a body of work by individual contributors or tell stories longer than was possible in the magazine. The 'One-Shots' were as successfully received as *Raw* itself and are now collectors' items. They were sold through bookshops, thereby increasing their distribution and promoting the acceptability of comics in mainstream publishing.

FRANÇOISE MOULY AND ART SPIEGELMAN (*b.*1948) eds.

Raw.
New York: Raw Books 1980–present.
v., ill.
ISSN 0742-4434.
Pressmark: COP.95.0055

Maus

ART SPIEGELMAN
(b.1948)

Maus: a survivor's tale.
New York: Pantheon
Books 1986.
159 p., chiefly ill.
ISBN 0394747232.
Pressmark: RAK.144

Maus tells the true story of the author's father, Vladek Spiegelman: of his experience as a Holocaust survivor and of his son's problematic relationship with him. The highly personal narrative alternates between the recent past of the 1970s and '80s, wherein the father–son relationship is depicted as Art interviews Vladek in preparation for creating *Maus,* and the historical past of the father's story: of his experience as a Polish Jew suffering Nazi persecution which led to incarceration in Auschwitz. Always interested in formal experiment, Spiegelman told this most serious of tales using the most basic and childlike of comic-book genres, the anthropomorphic cartoon strip. Here the Jews were cast as mice and the Nazis as cats.

Born in Stockholm in 1948, Art Spiegelman grew up in Rego Park, New York City, the son of Polish immigrant parents. A major figure in American 'alternative' comics, his style varies considerably from project to project as he pursues a post-modernist approach to the medium.

Maus originally appeared between 1980 and 1986, serialised as a child-sized supplement in the highly influential comics anthology magazine *Raw* (see p.136). Its success rocketed when it was subsequently published in 1986–87 in graphic-novel form under the title *Maus: a survivor's tale* by Pantheon/Penguin. A sequel, *Maus II: and here my troubles began*, appeared under the same imprint in 1992. In 1994 it was republished in CD-ROM format by The Voyager Company. This new edition includes detailed background information on the extensive research which Spiegelman undertook in the course of developing the project, which was 13 years in the preparation.

The strip stands as a powerfully direct, accessible and honest document about the difficulties facing Spiegelman's generation of American Jews in coming to terms with an increasingly distant and alienating past. *Maus* is a remarkable addition to the canon of work on the Holocaust, and won a Pulitzer Prize in 1992.

Watchmen

Watchmen, the very influential comic written by Alan Moore and illustrated by Dave Gibbons, received high critical acclaim for reinventing the superhero genre. The remarkable aspect of this attention was that it transcended the comics industry and fan press and, along with Frank Miller's *Dark Knight Returns*, was reviewed in serious literature pages as an example of a new maturity in superhero comics. Moore and Gibbons were graduates of British comics, both having worked on titles such as *Doctor Who Weekly* and *2000 AD*, moving on to the more adult titles of the early 1980s, and then to DC Comics in America. Alan Moore had already won awards for his work on *V for vendetta* and *Swamp Thing*.

Originally issued by DC Comics as a 12-part monthly comic book from October 1986, *Watchmen* was subsequently collected as a trade paperback, and it is in this graphic-novel format that it achieved wide notoriety. It is set in a contemporary New York where the presence of superheroes, in particular, the godlike Dr Manhattan, has altered history. The Cold War is at its nervous height, but the balance has been tipped so much in the United States' favour that the USSR is ready to launch a pre-emptive strike. The story follows Rorschach, a vigilante whose investigation into the murder of the Comedian tempts other superheroes out of retirement.

Watchmen makes great use of the genre conventions of superhero comic books. Origin stories are at least hinted at for all the superheroes featured, and much effort is made to fill in the background to invest the characters with a continuity. The advertisements often found in comic books are parodied, and a comic within a comic is even featured, commenting on the main storyline. The detailed artwork contrasts with a simple layout based on a grid of nine panels for each page. This was intended to draw the reader into the story and make the use of larger panels all the more dramatic. A full-page panel does not appear until the climax within the final chapter.

ALAN MOORE (*b*.1953) AND DAVE GIBBONS (*b*.1955) ill.

Watchmen.
New York: Warner Books 1987.
[413] p., col. ill.
ISBN 0446386898.
Pressmark:
COM.99.0005

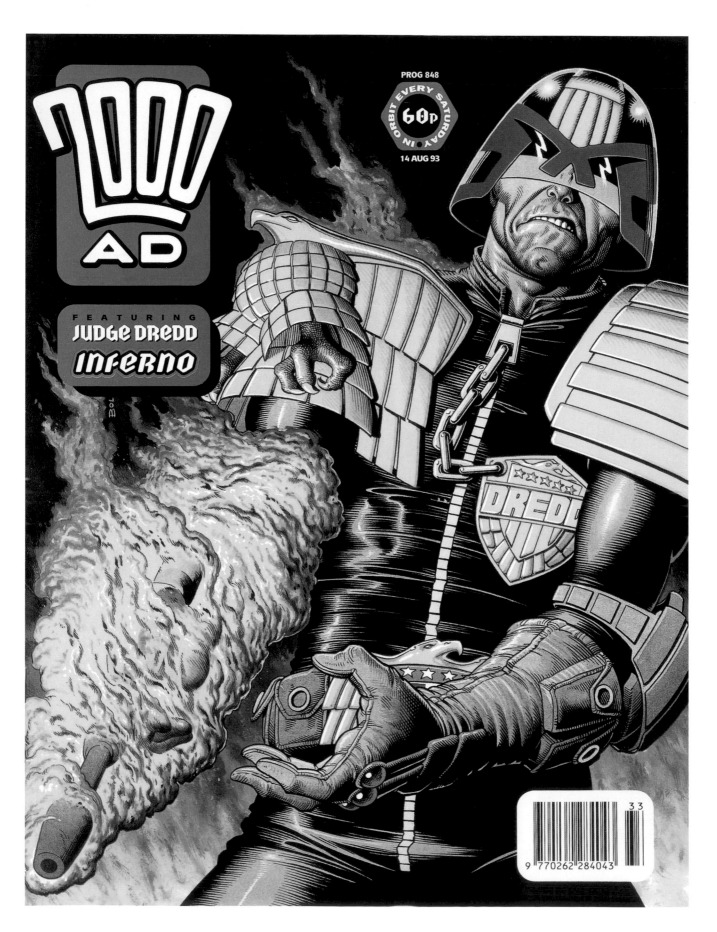

2000 AD

2000 AD

London: Fleetway
Editions 1977–
present. v., ill.
ISSN 0262-284X.
Pressmark:
COP.99.0023

2000 AD was launched on 26 February 1977 at a time, especially in the world of children's comics, when the millennium seemed a long way away.

The comic's origins lie in *Action,* a title previously published by IPC, Fleetway's parent company. This was a deliberate attempt to rethink boys' comics at a time when the market was in decline. The strips took their cue from contemporary adult and violent cinema and, controversially, challenged authority. Amidst inflammatory articles in the tabloid press, the title was suspended after less than a year, but not before IPC had noted its unprecedented level of sales and fanmail.

Much the same team of creators, led by Pat Mills, were involved in its successor, *2000 AD.* A science-fiction setting helped to avoid controversy, with more humour to soften the violence. More emphasis was placed in the visuals, with the layouts more flexible and American in style.

The new comic had a shaky start. It was merged with stable-mates *Starlord* and then *Tornado* before it found its niche. By 1982 the weekly circulation had reached a steady 120,000 copies and the fanmail showed the presence of a loyal audience in tune with the style of the comic. More remarkable was the profile of the readership. The comic's subversive humour and use of irony meant that it was not only retaining a section of its target audience as they grew older, but also gaining a significant adult readership. The lead character – Judge Dredd, 'Lawman of the Future' –

embodies this and has achieved international recognition in his own right.

Ironically, this period of success initiated a decline. *2000 AD*'s success with older readers presaged the adult comics boom of the mid-1980s, which tempted many readers away. The comic's policy of using, and crediting, British-based talent, made it a shop window for mainstream US publishers.

Confounding industry expectations, *2000 AD* has survived into the year 2000 itself. The success of many alumni has served to enhance the comic's reputation. A core loyal readership remains and now also sustains a companion title, *Judge Dredd Megazine,* launched in 1990.

7 Poetry and Experimental Typography

Typography, including both the design of typefaces and their selection and layout, is one of the fundamental book arts. However, unlike binding and book construction, or illustration and decoration, typography as such only came into being in the West in the mid-fifteenth century, as an integral part of the development of printing. Types were first designed to resemble scribal hands. This is evident in the 'black letter' or 'Gothic' styles still available today. But standard 'Roman' typefaces also derive from writing styles, those of the 'humanist' scribes in early Renaissance Italy. These had a clear line suitable to inked type, and were associated with the new revival of classical literature, so they became the basis for the development of types specifically adapted to the new medium, which took on its own aesthetic characteristics.

The National Art Library has never specifically set out to make a representative historical collection of typography; nevertheless its history of acquisitions has resulted in ownership of many early books noteworthy for their typography and printing, including 172 incunabula (books printed before 1500), with examples by celebrated printers such as Nicholas Jenson and Aldus Manutius. As publishing was then organised, it was the printers who were responsible for commissioning types, and whose discrimination thus contributed to their refinement.

The Library has, however, deliberately acquired examples of excellent contemporary book production (especially British) ever since its foundation in the mid-nineteenth century.

This was a period of great change in publishing, with the growth in literacy, the industrial mechanisation of printing, and the adoption of paper based on wood-pulp rather than cotton rag. Alongside the boom in literature, the quality of the physical book declined, in reaction to which there began towards the end of the century a revival of fine printing – largely influenced by William Morris – and a group of 'private presses' was established in Britain. The Library has a strong collection of such high-quality revivalist printing.

Meanwhile, the commercial possibilities of print were being explored further in advertising. 'Graphic design' developed: a new discipline marrying word and image. Influences pass to and fro between fine and applied arts: the ubiquity and impact of the typographic word in public spaces and the press was referred to by poets such as Stéphane Mallarmé, Guillaume Apollinaire and Paul van Ostaijen, and literally appropriated in the Cubists' paintings and collages, and in the art and printworks of the Futurists, Dadaists and Kurt Schwitters, which in turn influenced the school of 'new typography' founded in the 1920s at the Bauhaus in Berlin. Bauhaus-derived type styles – minimalist, sanserif, eschewing upper case – are characteristic of much concrete and other poetry (for example, that of Eugen Gomringer). The NAL has large collections of 'jobbing printing', commercial printed ephemera mainly of the 1930s and 1960s, containing work by distinguished graphic designers and typographers such as El Lissitsky, Eric Gill, Jan Tschichold and Piet Zwart, as well as many typical, generic items designed to grab attention, in a print-busy world.

In this chapter, typography in the National Art Library is represented by a selection of works by poets who have extended their literary intention to the look and arrangement of the letters and words on the page. The field could be extended to include collaborations between writers and designers/typographers, and books combining typography with images made in other media; indeed the *Prose du Transsibérien* in Chapter 8 (p. 166) falls into both categories. There is also an important class of book in which the writer's intention is transmitted by directly reproducing his or her handwriting in facsimile rather than its typographic translation: Matisse's *Jazz* (1947) is a famous example (see above, p. 69), and several of the writers illustrated here also published their work in this way. However, even restricting the focus as we have done, to purely typographic works either of poetry or by poets, where the writer was interested and able to specify typeface(s) and arrangement, the NAL contains a great diversity.

The works by Marinetti, Apollinaire, Terent'ev and van Ostaijen included here must be seen in the wider context of the early-twentieth century avant-garde Movements, principally Futurism and Dadaism, that encompassed all the arts, and to varying degrees, social and political activism too. The progressive artist's work came to encompass discourse, often propagandist, *about* the art (an idea discussed further in Chapter 8), and typographic experimentation was associated with opposition to mainstream taste and attitudes. There was a proliferation of artist-run, graphically innovative periodicals: *Lacerba*, Theo van Doesburg's *De Stijl*, the various manifestations of *Dada*, Stieglitz's and Picabia's *291* and *391*, Kurt Schwitters's *Merz*. Of these, the National Art Library has representative, if not comprehen-

sive, holdings. Likewise, most of the items illustrated here were self-published: artists and writers directly controlled their means of production and could thus, within financial limitations (and occasionally subject to censorship), control all aspects of their appearance and content.

Among the literary arts, poetry is by convention typographically distinctive, being set in lines that correspond to metrical verses, or with free verse – another nineteenth-century development – to phrasal measures. Thus it tends to retain a visual relationship to its aural delivery, including, as in *Un coup de dés ...* and Gomringer's 'schweigen', the dramatisation of silence. There is a persistent, and at first sight paradoxical, relationship between visual poetry, which might be expected to have its total life on the page, and performance; this tradition is reinforced by John Cage's use, as a composer, of typography to function *as* music and finds its radical continuation in the late work of Bob Cobbing.

From the mid-twentieth century, typesetting and reproductive technology was not only within poets' budgets, but available to non-expert operators: after typewriters and stencil-based duplicators came Letraset and Xerox: do-it-yourself publishing was open to all. These developments are represented in the Library's holdings of concrete poetry from the 1960s and early '70s, as well as copier and mail art and fanzines from the 1980s onwards. Computer-based word-processing and desktop-publishing facilitated such activities, but it is the World Wide Web, developed in the early 1990s, which looks as if it will change publishing and communications as profoundly as did the invention of printing. Type and graphic designers are busy creating products expressly for screen display, but writers and artists are also becoming more involved in the design for online publication of their own work, making it at once more accessible – and less collectible.

Double Dice

'Un coup de dés jamais n'abolira le hasard' (1897) by Stéphane Mallarmé inaugurated a new awareness among writers and artists of the expressive possibilities of typography and the printed page, partly influenced by the look of commercial press and advertising layout and graphic design. There are dramatic variations in type size, lines are often spread across the double page opening, and the words of the title thread independently throughout the whole poem. From its ostensible subject, a shipwreck, the poem philosophises on the hazards of decision and action. Mallarmé's fellow poet Paul Valéry recollected seeing it for the first time:

> It seemed to me that I was looking at the form and pattern of a thought, placed for the first time in finite space ... Expectancy, doubt, concentration, all were *visible things* ... Inappreciable instants became clearly visible; the fraction of a second during which an idea flashes into being and dies away.

The poem, Mallarmé's last, was first published in 1897, though not until 1914, sixteen years after the poet's death, did a version appear that exactly followed his instructions as to type sizes and placing on the page. 'A cast of dice never can annul chance' translates the poem into English while also following those instructions, newly researched from Mallarmé's own annotated proofs (now in the Houghton Library, Harvard University); it gives the non-Francophone an experience very close to that of reading the original. This book is a collaboration between the translator and the artist/publisher, Ian Tyson, who also contributes plates, geometric abstracts in rich black aquatint which complement the suggestive, undecidable mood of the poem, visually reversing its proportion of white to black, perhaps further to explore the idea of what in painting would be called the 'negative space' between significant forms. It is clear that this is a sympathetic response: Mallarmé himself wrote (in his essay on Poe),

> The intellectual armature of the poem conceals itself and remains – happens – in the space which isolates the stanzas amid the white of the paper: meaningful silence, no less beautiful to compose than verses.

The version of 'Un coup de dés...' made by the Belgian conceptual artist and poet Marcel Broodthaers takes this notion to a logical conclusion: by replacing every line with printer's leading of the right height and length he literally silences the poem's words. For Mallarmé's subtitle, 'poème', he substitutes a new title: 'image.' Whether the intention is satire or homage is unclear; perhaps there are elements of both. Such ambiguity is characteristic of Broodthaers's work. However, he is quoted as saying 'Mallarmé is the source of contemporary art. He has unconsciously invented modern space....' The semi-transparency of the paper selected for this book results in several layers of 'show-through', a beautiful effect suggesting the text perhaps immersed in water, or seen receding into the distance.

STÉPHANE
MALLARMÉ
(1842–1898)

'A cast of dice never
can annul chance.'
Translation by Neil
Crawford; aquatints
by Ian Tyson.
London: Tetrad 1985.
[28] p., [4] leaves of
plates, ill.
Pressmark:
95.HH.1

MARCEL
BROODTHAERS
(1924–1976)

'Image: un coup de
dés jamais n'abolira
le hasard.'
Antwerp: Galerie
Wide White Space
1969. [25] leaves,
chiefly ill.
Pressmark:
G.28.Box.I.G

Simultaneity

'Lettre-Océan' was the first published poem by Guillaume Apollinaire to incorporate typographic experimentation. It originally appeared in the review magazine *Les Soirées de Paris,* of which Apollinaire himself was a co-founder and editor, in June 1914. It was followed in the July/August issue by four more shaped poems, initially dubbed *idéogrammes lyriques* and which Apollinaire later renamed *calligrammes.*

The magazine had been founded in 1912 by friends of Apollinaire, in an attempt to lift his spirits after a false arrest, and brief incarceration on suspicion of complicity in a theft from the Louvre. Despite some opposition, Apollinaire used the magazine to promote the 'new painting', particularly Cubism. When the magazine changed hands in September 1913 Apollinaire was allowed to promulgate his writings on avant-garde artists unimpeded.

Apollinaire's close association with avant-garde artists was to have a profound effect on his poetry, as lyricism gave way to a period of experimentation in both the form and content of his work. For Apollinaire the modern work of art should reflect contemporary urban consciousness, characterised by the simultaneous awareness of a multiplicity of fragmented but related perceptions and sensations. In poetry this could only be achieved by a radical departure from a linear, discursive structure where each line is read and understood successively, in favour of *simultaneism:* a structure in which ideas and perceptions are randomly juxtaposed. The reader, reassembling them into a new order, achieves an instant awareness that approximates simultaneous consciousness. 'Lettre-Océan'

moved one step further, abandoning a traditional linear layout in an effort to convey an instant awareness 'synthetico-ideographically', that is through visual as well as verbal means.

Within the ostensible framework of a letter posted at sea (and including perhaps the idea of a surging ocean of sensation and of 'letters', correspondent and literary), 'Lettre-Océan' evokes a world of global communication and technological advances. The two central motifs of radiating lines represent the Eiffel Tower, identified in the first circle by its geographical location, in the second by its height, 'Sur la rive gauche devant le pont d'Iéna', and 'Haute de 300 mètres', the radio waves departing from its transmitters made up of overheard snippets of conversation and a series of onomatopoeic sound impressions.

GUILLAUME
APOLLINAIRE
(1880–1918)

'Lettre-Océan'
[Ocean-Letter],
Les Soirées de Paris
no. 25, 15 June 1914,
pp. [340–41].
Pressmark: 95.CC.30

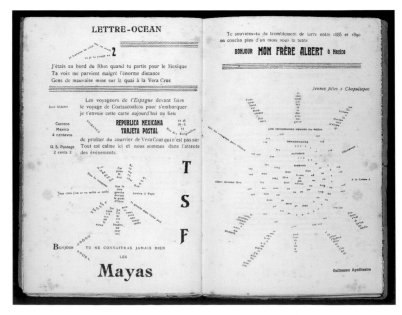

Words in Freedom

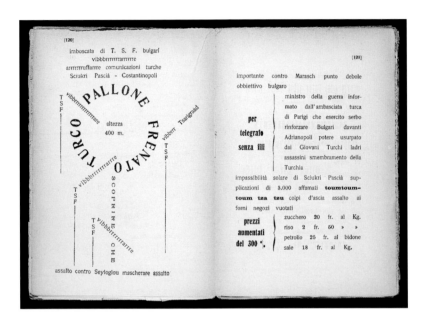

FILIPPO
TOMMASO
MARINETTI
(1876–1944)

*Zang tumb tuuum:
Adrianopoli, ottobre
1912: Parole in
libertà.*
Milano: Edizioni
futuriste di 'Poesia'
1914. 225 p.
Pressmark: SP.91.0004

It was a poet, F.T. Marinetti, who established the style and strategy of a whole series of twentieth-century avant-garde Movements, when he invented Futurism at a stroke in 1909 with the publication of a manifesto. The manifesto, previously associated with political rhetoric, instantly became established as a form of literature, often more successful as such than the poetry and art whose ideas it ostensibly promoted. The second distinctive literary form of Futurism was completely new: a variety of poetry called *parole in libertà*: words-in-freedom. This book collects two of Marinetti's manifestos together with an extended exercise in words-in-freedom as a bold demonstration piece.

Words-in-freedom are concrete, paratactic and onomatopoeic, with adjectives used as if they were nouns, and verbs primarily in the infinitive. The combining mechanisms, by which words become more or less transparent 'signifiers', are cut away, words are treated as *things*. It follows that punctuation is abandoned, words are set widely spaced to fit the shape of the page, in variegated typefaces and styles, and non-verbal typographic signs, especially mathematical symbols, are employed as if they were text items. Marinetti declared a 'revolution... aimed at the so-called harmony of the page'; in fact an almost sculptural sensibility is revealed in the tightly controlled but flexibly varied page design of this book. Its intrinsic value perhaps lies more in this than the device of typographic icons, such as the 'balloon' here, or Marinetti's 'crude and brutal' (his own words) vocal imitations of battle sounds. White space is dramatically enclosed within the bold, rectilinear text field, reversing the usual proportions. Contrast, for example, 'Un coup de dés ...' (p. 147): Marinetti disparaged Mallarmé's 'decorative, precious aesthetic'.

The subject matter is far from abstract, however: a war report, from first-hand observation, of the Bulgarian siege of Adrianopolis in Turkey, complete with facts and figures. It was innovative to treat such a text as poetry; it also confronts us with the amoral exhilaration of the Futurist's response to modern applications of technology to communications, transport and warfare: the latter, in Marinetti's repellent doctrine, 'the world's only hygiene'.

Стих 1.　Вотъ къ сожалѣнію дошли мы до черт знаетъ какой **МУД**ости!

Начинается блаженство учениковъ и ни въ чемъ неповинныя жертвы.

Мы въ кафэ сидимъ какъ три митрополита, три папы, три бабы, три зуба:

Крученыхъ, Зданевичъ и Терентьевъ!!!

Стих 2.　Вотъ нѣкоторыя слова: упразднить, испраздить, исправить, правило, порожній, прахъ, на всѣхъ парахъ..... отсюда выводъ:

МЫ ПРА∞ДУ ма т КУ рубимъ потнЫе от счастья

ш ТОПОРЫ ФУ ТУ РИЗМА

(съ тѣхъ поръ, съ той поры, топоръ).

Утих 3.　Вопервыхъ — ⊏⊃⊂⊃⊃⊃⊃⊐⊃ ⊐⊃⊐⊃⊐ —самый крѣпкій и разнообразный: anglſчане говорятъ только на провалившемся языкѣ (Тифлисъ=Шифилисъ), italiанцы—высуня (bona сѣра), поляки на зубахъ (цикаво пшезъ дживи патшить), а французы—однѣми губами (Minion!) Русскій ничѣмъ не брезгаетъ: **Х**аркаетъ, **Ы**кота и высочайше **Ю**каетъ! Отсюда **ВСЕЛЕНСКОЕ ЗНАЧЕНІЕ** русской ругани:—верхній регистръ! Елки палки! И нижайшее почтеніе на **Ы**: "упалъ на л**Ы**ки (Анчаръ).

Псих 4.　Слово fуtуrism—означаетъ поиноязычному свое нѣкоторое, а для насъ фютюр=фитюлька! Правильнѣе говорить: фу ты, ну ты, ножки гнуты,

Transrational Language

IGOR TERENT'EV
(1892–1941?)

Traktat o sploshnom neprilichii ['Tract of total obscenity'].
Tblisi: Kompaniia 41°
[1920]. 15 p.
Pressmark:
36.C Box III (xxviii)

Igor Terent'ev's 'Tract of Total Obscenity' is a rare manifesto of Russian Futurism. Both the literary genre and the typography show the influence of Italian Futurism (Marinetti visited Moscow and St Petersburg in 1914) but the Russian Movement had a distinct origin and development, from literary Symbolism and visual Impressionism and Cubism.

The *Traktat* was published in Tiflis (Tblisi), capital of Georgia, which for several years following the Russian Revolution, and the subsequent civil war, became a refuge for many artists and writers, who, like Terent'ev, had formerly been active in Moscow and St Petersburg. The imprint is '41°', an enterprise consisting of Terent'ev himself together with fellow poets A. Kruchenykh, a prolific literary activist and publisher, and Ilya Zdanevich. (The names of all three appear here at line 7, in italics, 'sitting in a cafe like ... three popes, three old ladies, three teeth' – and with three exclamation marks). Zdanevich was the one with typographic expertise: he later took the imprint to Paris, and, as 'Iliazd', created and published *livres d'artistes* in collaboration with artists and writers including Max Ernst and Picasso. It is likely then that the appearance of this book owes much to him.

A good deal is communicated by the page, even to a reader without Russian. The mixture of type sizes and faces, including Roman script, visually suggests an aural and multilingual cacophony, in which sounds and puns are prioritised over meaning. A high degree of parallelism or rhyme is visible: uprazdnit, isprazdnit, ispravit, pravilo (i.e. celebrate,

defecate ... regulation, etc, line 8). Words are invented and disassembled until the reader is ready to see that for instance Futurizma ('Futurism', line 25) contains both turizm ('tourism'), and tuz ('ace card', 'big shot'). Type is rotated sideways: the 'B' in pravdu ('truth', line 11) absurdly suggesting buttocks. Language is pushed beyond sense: this kind of writing was highly developed among the Russian Futurist poets, who called it 'zaumist' or 'transrational'; here the eclectic typography expresses its linguistic unconventionality. Terent'ev further argues that thus deconstructed, language inevitably betrays 'indecent' double-entendres – a perception undoubtedly influenced by Freudian theory. Russian is claimed as superior among languages, in particular the 'universal meaning' (vselenskoe znachenie) of Russian obscenities, asserted irreverently in the decorative script of Church Slavic.

Rhythmic Typography

Expressive typography achieves an artistic maturity that transcends novelty or sensationalism in this substantial book by Paul van Ostaijen, who was a short-lived but precocious writer from the Flemish region of Belgium. The poem-cycle concerns the German occupation ('bezetting') of his native city, Antwerp, during the First World War; like T.S. Eliot's 'The Waste Land' (1922), it addresses the disintegration of personal and cultural continuities in Europe at that era with a stylistic montage, but it carries the theme further into technique by visibly fragmenting the text across the whole space of the page. The subject matter is often sombre, as in the poem illustrated, which deals with the anxiety of waiting for letters from sons and brothers at the Front; visually nevertheless the book communicates a certain metropolitan exhilaration.

In a lengthy defence of his self-styled 'rhythmic typography', van Ostaijen wrote that he intended it as a visual correlative for actual utterance, the poem 'speaking itself'. One reason why this Modernist classic is not better known may be that it is written in Dutch, one of Europe's minority languages. Van Ostaijen was active in the Flemish cultural revival of the period; but his essays and journalism also attempted to infuse the local with the contemporary international cultural currents of Cubism, Futurism and Expressionism. Paradoxically, at the end of the War he left Antwerp for Berlin, fearing a Francophone backlash against Flemish activists who had been abetted by the Germans – and it was there that *Bezette Stad* was written,

alongside both *Der Sturm* Expressionism, with its dramatic style in book design, and German Dada, with its characteristic verbal and typographic disruptiveness.

The cover design and illustrations, abstract constructions based on typographic shapes, are by Oskar Jespers, one of van Ostaijen's many artist-friends. Also closely involved with the book's production was the lawyer René Victor, a supporter and patron of their artistic circle. The imprint, Het Sienjaal, is the title of an earlier volume of van Ostaijen's poems.

PAUL VAN OSTAIJEN (1896–1928) AND OSKAR JESPERS

Bezette stad. Originaalhoutsneden en tekeningen van Oskar Jespers. Antwerp: Sienjaal 1921. [153] p., ill. Pressmark: 95.JJ.35

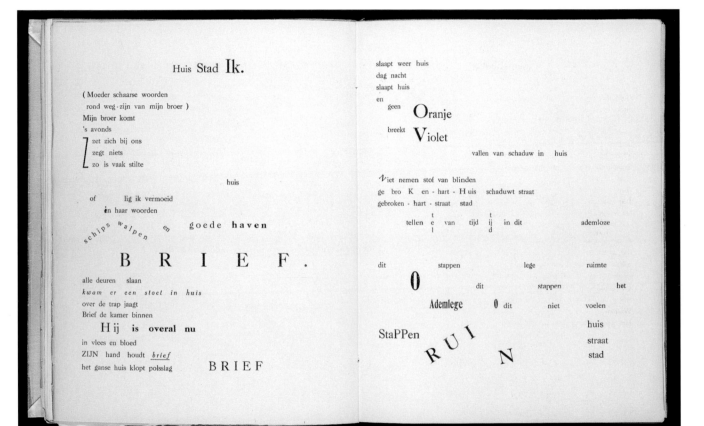

Huis Stad Ik.

(Moeder schaarse woorden
rond weg - zijn van mijn broer)
Mijn broer komt
's avonds
⌈ zet zich bij ons
| zegt niets
⌊ zo is vaak stilte

huis

of   lig ik vermoeid
in haar woorden

schipz walpen   en   goede haven

B R I E F.

alle deuren   slaan
kwam er een stoet in huis
over de trap jaagt
Brief de kamer binnen
Hij   is   overal   nu
in vlees en bloed
ZIJN hand houdt *brief*
het ganse huis klopt polsslag   BRIEF

slaapt weer huis
dag nacht
slaapt huis
en
    geen   Oranje
breekt   Violet
                    vallen van schaduw in   huis

Viet nemen stof van blinden
ge bro K en - hart - H uis   schaduwt straat
gebroken - hart - straat   stad
                    t   t
tellen   e van   tijd ij in dit   ademloze
                    l   d

dit   stappen   lege   ruimte
                    0   dit   stappen   het
        Ademlege   0 dit   niet   voelen
                                                    huis
StaPPen   RUIN   straat
                    N   stad

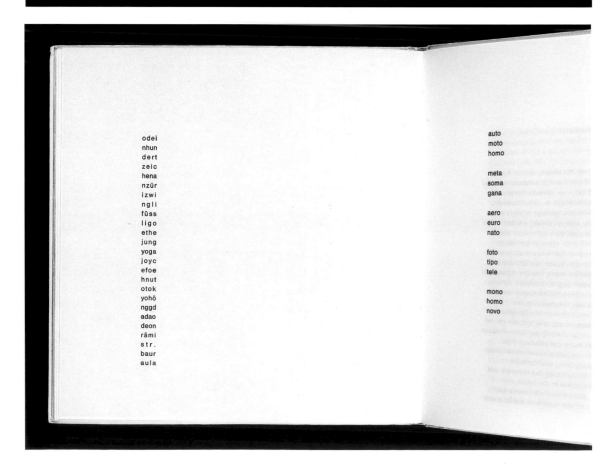

avenidas
avenidas y flores

flores
flores y mujeres

avenidas
avenidas y mujeres

avenidas y flores y mujeres y
un admirador

odei
nhun
dert
zeic
hena
nzür
izwi
ngli
füss
ligo
ethe
jung
yoga
joyc
efoe
hnut
otok
yohö
nggd
adao
deon
rămi
str.
baur
aula

auto
moto
homo

meta
soma
gana

aero
euro
nato

foto
tipo
tele

mono
homo
novo

Concrete Poetry: 'Constellations'

EUGEN
GOMRINGER
(*b*.1925)

33 konstellationen.
St Gallen: Tschudy
Verlag 1960.
[48] p., col. ill.
(Quadrat-bücher; 11)
Pressmark:
G.29.W.131

Eugen Gomringer is a founder of the international Concrete Poetry Movement; this book includes some of his earliest and most famous poems, written in the early 1950s, before the Movement had technically begun. For Gomringer, the 'constellation', a brief, concentrated word-cluster, was allied to other modern forms of abbreviated verbal communication, 'as easily understood as ... traffic signs'. It should be a purposeful structure, like architecture: 'It is a reality in itself and not a poem about something or other.' This is the sense in which it is 'concrete'.

The term 'Art concret' had been used by Theo van Doesburg, the painter and co-founder of De Stijl, in 1930, advocating abstraction, clarity and an anti-sentimental, constructivist approach. Gomringer was influenced by his contacts with artists in this tradition, notably Max Bill, whose secretary he became from 1954 to 1958; Bill contributed several images to *33 konstellationen*. From 1955 to 1956 Gomringer entered into an alliance in the name of 'concrete poetry' with a group of Brazilian poets, the 'Noigandres'; meanwhile, in Sweden, the term had been independently coined by another poet, Öyvind Fahlström. The Movement gained momentum quickly, and was promulgated in periodicals and a series of anthologies and exhibitions.

Gomringer's own poems are visually distinctive for their typographic and verbal minimalism, a style widely adopted by other poets of the movement. Lines, words or individual letters may be arranged to create shapes on the page, but his cool, understated style contrasts with Apollinaire's pictorialism or Futurist 'words-in-freedom'.

The international aspect of concrete poetry was part of its vitality, its visual emphasis and often simple vocabulary rendering work in different languages relatively accessible. Gomringer, born in Bolivia, though brought up in Zürich, wrote 'avenida y flores', the very first 'constellation', in Spanish, his mother-tongue. The permuting procedure of this piece was repeated frequently, by himself and other poets. The 'ode in a hundred signs' lists items relating to the city of 'züri[ch]', including Jung, James Joyce and Dada. The celebrated one-word 'schweigen' ('silence') enacts its meaning by erasure; it works in any language.

Poetry in Colour

Rapel is the first book of concrete poetry by the Scottish poet-artist Ian Hamilton Finlay. Finlay began his career quite conventionally writing fairly successful short stories, one-act plays and lyric poems; he was as surprised as anyone by the change in his work:

> 'Concrete' began for me with the extraordinary (since wholly unexpected) sense that the syntax I had been using, *the movement* of language in me, at a physical level, was no longer there – so it had to be replaced with something else, with a syntax and movement that would be true of the new feeling (which existed in only the vaguest way, since I had, then, no form for it...).

Though Finlay may not at first have known of the other poets working in the same vein, the subtitle of this book indicates his awareness of earlier currents in the visual arts, from whom he might borrow approaches both to expression and to visual design.

By the time of *Rapel*, however, Finlay was in contact with other concrete poets in Europe, the United States and South America, and furthered the movement himself by publishing many of them in his magazine, *Poor. Old. Tired. Horse* (1961 or '62 to 1967 or '68). He had also co-founded the press, Wild Hawthorn, which eventually came to publish all his own work.

Rapel is a blend of modesty and luxury in presentation. It consists of ten quarto cardboard sheets in a card folder, and the style has a restraint like Eugen Gomringer's 'clean' con-crete; however, it uses a range of faces and, unusually for a book of poems, is printed in two, and in places, three colours. The poem illustrated employs the visual qualities of letters typographically rendered, as well as insisting on their sounds, to depict a pastoral scene – but a working landscape, be it noted – synaesthetically. The repeated 'm' shapes and sounds image ripples, voice the connection between stream and mill, and also simply murmur with pleasure.

IAN HAMILTON
FINLAY (*b.*1925)

Rapel: 10 fauve and suprematist poems.
Edinburgh: Wild Hawthorn Press 1963.
1 folder (11 sheets).
Pressmark:
95.W Box II

m
Mm
x
m
mMm
x
m
mm
m
mm
x
MmM
mm
m
m
mm
m
x
mmm
m
m
mm
x
m
mmMm
m
x
m
mm
m
this
is
the
little
burn
that
plays
its
mm
mMm
m
mmouth-
organ
by
the
m
mm
mmm
mMm
mill
x
mm
Mmm

i h f

Jehanne la bonne Lorraine
Jeanne la bonne Lorraine
Je anne La bonne Lorr
Jehannnne   nnn   Lorrr   anglois brulerent
Jehann   NNNNNNNN   Lorrrr
Jehanne NNNNNNNN   Lorrr
ehann   NNNNNNNN   ooo   Orr
Jehanne Jeahhane Jeanne
Jehanne Heahnne   lorraine
Jehanne   reine
        bonne   rein
Je anne bonne la reine
Jehanne bonne   reine
Je anne bonne   reine
Jeh anne bonne Lorraine
J   anne la bonne rraine
J   hanne la bonne
J ehann rein Lorraine
J ehann rein Lorraine
    nnn rein Lorr
J ehanne la bonne Lorraine
Jeh anni la bonne Lorrai
    ha la la   Lorr
        la la   orraine
Jehanne la la   orraine
Jehanne   onne
           nn
Jehanne la nn   rrr
        la bonne Lorraine
J annnnn onne Lorraine
I nnnn   n   rr
Je anne la onne Lorraine

anglois brulerent

Poetry of the Machine

ILSE (*b.*1928) AND
PIERRE (*b.*1927)
GARNIER

*Othon III, Jeanne
d'Arc: structures
historiques.*
[Paris]: Éditions André
Silvaire [1967?]. 1 v.
(Collection
'Spatialisme')
Pressmark
310. J Box.II

This book is an ambitious experiment in applying the means of concrete poetry to historical narrative. Visually, it stands for a great number of small press books and magazines in the 1960s and '70s, reproduced directly from typescript by some form of office duplicator. For Pierre Garnier, the 'machine à écrire' was indispensable to the production of the 'mechanical poem' ('poème mécanique') that he wanted: 'Under the fingers' impulse the keys beat the ribbon, which by percussion prints the white page.' Some concrete poets, notably Dom Sylvester Houédard and Henri Chopin, were typewriter virtuosi, producing dazzling optical 'typestracts' (Houédard's term). The Garniers' work is less perfectionist; their engagement with elaborate subject matter also contrasts with the self-contained immediacy of much other concrete poetry.

The Emperor Othon, or Otto, III dreamed of restoring Rome's former pre-eminence. A classicist and theologian, he made and unmade popes before dying on campaign in Italy in 1002 at the age of 22. Garnier is interested in the 'surreal' times around the first millennium, and in the image of 'the free hero [as] form and function of the free universe', a notion perhaps extrapolated from Existentialism, the French philosophy so influential in the mid-twentieth century. Garnier's philosophy is 'Spatialism': Spatialist writing he characterises as integral, untranslatable, supranational. Like Otto, Garnier imagines a new universal empire, but in poetry.

The thematic link between Otto and the better-known Joan of Arc (Ilse Garnier's part of the book) is the confrontation and inter-mingling of power-politics with religious faith in two very brief lives, one French, one German (the nationalities of Pierre and Ilse Garnier respectively). This page deals with Joan's burning by the English at Rouen, quoting François Villon's poem 'Testament' ('Jehanne la bonne Lorraine / qu'Englois brulerent à Rouan'). At a vertical 'stake' created by the unvarying implacability of cruelty, the human being is breaking up, with cries, moans ('NNNNNNNN OOO') and the lamentations ('la la') of others, but it is also an apotheosis: Jehane's lonely 'ein' becoming 'reine', a queen, her still-contained openness rising above the repetitive war-cry opposite.

Word – Score – Choreography

Sixty-two mesostics... is part of a small collection in the National Art Library of visual music scores, by John Cage and others. Composers in the 1950s – contemporary with the birth of concrete poetry – began experimenting with non-standard notations, either to increase expressive possibilities or to involve performers more in the composition. Cage was an influential writer, poet and graphic artist, as well as composer; this work was made to honour his long-time collaborator, the dancer and choreographer Merce Cunningham. It was composed – in days before computerised typesetting and pagemaking – with transfer letters, using more than 700 different typefaces and sizes.

A 'mesostic' is a word or text found by reading single letters from successive words in a base text or word list. Cage makes his mesostics by applying his subject's name, letter by letter, to a collection of source texts: 32 books from Cunningham's library, plus his *Changes: notes on choreography* (1969), a book itself unconventional in structure and layout, whose title reflects the interest Cunningham shared with Cage in the Chinese divinatory text *I-Ching*, or Book of Changes. Both men utilised it, and other 'chance' procedures, to generate art, music or dance.

It is possible to source a few fragments of Cage's texts in Cunningham's book, and their vocabulary includes references of interest to both men, e.g. botany, dance and Zen Buddhism. But the number of books used, and the chance-derived selection of words, or even parts of words, sometimes recombined together, make it impossible to 'solve' these mesostics by external reference. The typography further obscures or at least delays legibility – we experience each first as a kind of *Gestalt* image-impression, 'like a single cry', as Cage's notes have it – but it also returns us to them as a score 'for voice unaccompanied using microphone', where '*to read* becomes the verb *to sing*'. At once distinctive and indeterminate, their subject is, essentially, Cunningham himself, his name threaded through them, in a creative act of dedication.

JOHN CAGE
(1912-1992)

Sixty-two mesostics re Merce Cunningham. New York: Henmar Press 1971. 62 p. Pressmark: 82.E Box V (3)

41.

Visual Poetry

BOB COBBING
(b.1920)

A surplus of unsaleable beauty. Theme by Lawrence Upton. London: Writers Forum 1999. [8] p., chiefly ill. ([Domestic ambient noise]). ISBN 0861628780.

More than any of the other books illustrated in this chapter, this visual text challenges our definition of what poetry is.

Bob Cobbing became involved in experimental art and writing in the 1950s; by the 1960s he was prominent in the Concrete Poetry Movement, and especially active in performing and recording its oral equivalent, 'sound poetry'. He has worked extensively with free-improvising musicians, and with his wife, artist and dancer Jennifer Pike, and developed a very open view of what is performable: anything visual can, in his view, be voiced, or indeed danced.

Alongside his commitment to the human voice Cobbing has always emphasised the use – or, as he puts it, the misuse – of technology, usually the kind of 'low-fi' equipment available to the underfunded: Gestetner duplicators, cassette tape recorders, latterly the photocopier. These are not merely means to reproduction and distribution but essential media in their own right. Here Cobbing's work bears some relation to that of copier artists; using all kinds of objects and images on the platen he achieves a remarkable range of textures and depth effects. However, although the results often look like pure image, words are generally referenced or hinted somewhere – in a fleeting smear at the bottom of the page here, for instance. This, together with Cobbing's lineage and his continued presentation of the work as books of poetry to be read, leads us to include it as an example of radical typography.

Writers Forum, established in 1954, is Cobbing's own prolific imprint; this, according to the ISBN, is its 878th title. The 'Domestic Ambient Noise' series is its largest project: a six-year collaboration of visual poetry in 300 pamphlets, between Cobbing and fellow-poet Lawrence Upton, each part consisting of a set of variations by one, on a 'theme' provided by the other. This issue also commemorates the recent display in the National Art Library of another Writers Forum publication (Betty Radin's *Writers Blocks)* from which Upton's 'theme' page is adapted.

8 Book Art

Man's recorded history has seen a very wide variety of methods of conveying textual information. Although moveable type was invented in eleventh-century China, it was Caxton and Gutenberg's similar invention in the fifteenth century which resulted in a format which has since then proved phenomenally popular.

In ancient times, 4 to 3000 BC, the clay tablet was a popular method of conveying and recording household information and diplomatic messages. It was also used to record texts such as the Mesopotamian *Epic of Gilgamesh*. These clay tablets were in different formats: oblong, square, or sometimes, as in the case of tablets used in the nineteenth to sixteenth centuries BC for divination rites, in the form of a sheep's liver. At the same time, information was recorded in less portable form as inscriptions on the walls of the Egyptian pyramids and other monumental structures.

Later, leather, parchment and copper were all used to make scrolls, such as the 800 Dead Sea Scrolls, dating back more than 2000 years, which were found in 1947. An inscription on black basalt stone, the so-called Rosetta stone, made *c*.196 BC and rediscovered in the 1790s during Napoleon's survey of Egypt, provided us with the essential key to understanding Egyptian hieroglyphs. Animal bones were used as far afield as China and Egypt for inscription. Mother-of-pearl inlays in wood have been used, as have engravings on precious stones, and inscriptions on cotton cloth, all to record human activity in textual format.

Over the last 500 years or so, the most popular format for such work has been the codex: moveable type printed on paper, and sewn or glued together between outer boards. However, the turn of the last century saw the beginnings of experimentation with this format, a movement led by artists. In fact, a significant feature of the latter part of the twentieth century was the creation of books as works of art in themselves. Some of these artworks were produced by people who came from a background of traditional activities associated with books, such as binding, book illustration or design; while others were made by artists who wished to explore the role of books in daily life and in our culture generally. They provide a forceful comment on the association that books have for the individual and society.

But what exactly is an artist's book and what is meant by 'book art'? Simon Ford has collected some 27 definitions, ranging from those which declare that only cheap books in editions of thousands of copies can be regarded as artist's books (a definition conforming to a political agenda which resents the imposition of art dealers and museums and galleries between the artist and the person experiencing the artwork), to unique works – an edition of one.

The Art Libraries Society of the United Kingdom and Ireland (ARLIS/UK & Ireland) produced a definition for the practical purpose of identifying such books for special descriptive treatment when recording a library's holdings: 'a book or book-like object in which an artist has had a major input beyond illustration or authorship: where the final appearance of the book owes much to an artist's interference/participation: where the book is the manifestation of the artist's creativity: where the book is a work of art in itself.'

The National Art Library has long collected books disseminating the ideas of artists and demonstrating the artist's experimentation with the medium of the book. The current collection, some 5,000 items, dates from the 1890s and includes some fine examples from the first half of the twentieth century, with many great names from the period represented – Picasso, Kokoschka, Vuillard, Dali, Bonnard, Matisse, and more recently Jean Dubuffet, Tom Phillips, Francesco Clemente and David Hockney. Many of these works were included in an exhibition mounted by the National Art Library in 1985, *From Manet to Hockney: modern artists' illustrated books*. These artists' books – also known as *livres d'artistes* – were mostly produced as traditional books, albeit at the more expensive end of the cost spectrum.

Compared to these works, however, it is generally accepted that the conceptual work of Ed Ruscha and Dieter Roth in the 1960s marked the foundation of a new trend of experimentation, which resulted in the 1980s and 1990s in a massive increase of artists using the book as a medium of self-expression. While small presses and individuals continued to promote the art of letterpress printing and the hand-crafted book, many artists took up the challenge to experiment with the physical structure of the traditional book form. 'Book-Works', as they are sometimes called, step outside conventional boundaries associated with books to encompass concepts previously more closely associated with the fine arts. These works range from the minuscule to the gargantuan, and sometimes take the form of installation pieces. A 'book-work' is no longer restricted to paper and ink; all kinds of materials and appended objects may be incorporated. While such works are usually unique, or in a very limited edition, some artists have succeeded in producing multiple copies of their works in unlimited editions.

These books, which experiment with the traditional format of the book, are themselves works of art, and are sometimes called 'Book Art'. As a genre they challenge one's concept of what reading is, since, in many cases, conventional text has completely disappeared.

In recent years the National Art Library has concentrated on building up its collection of contemporary artists' book-works, and now contains the largest collection of such works in the British Isles. This collection of book art is international in scope and includes work from all Continents, although the largest representation is from the United States and Western Europe. Material included in the collection has been created from 1960 onwards.

Over the next few pages some examples from the NAL Collection are presented, the works illustrating how artists of the twentieth century have transformed word into image.

La prose du Transsibérien

At the beginning of the twentieth century a major Movement broke with past traditions of some 400 years and changed the ways in which books are made. This was an artistic prefiguration of what science would discover later in the twentieth century – the difference between the left brain and right brain; whilst the left brain looks at things consecutively, chronologically, sequentially, in series, the right brain looks at things simultaneously, in a *Gestalt,* perceiving the completed form. It accesses several different inputs at the same time and deals with non-verbal image recognition. This activity makes it possible to perceive two opposites at once, at a single glance, instantaneously. This discovery was prefigured at the beginning of the century in a great work of art by Sonia Delaunay and Blaise Cendrars.

The book consists of four sheets joined together and folded in half vertically and then concertinaed to form 42 sections, attached to a parchment cover painted in oil after a composition by Delaunay. When the book is unfolded it measures nearly 7 ft, with the right-hand side containing a poem by Cendrars, the left in parallel consisting of an abstract pochoir illumination in gouache and watercolour in brilliant colours by Delaunay. The text-side makes use of different-coloured inks and a variety of typefaces and experiments with typographical layout, the text sometimes justified on the right, sometimes on the left, and sometimes centred. The indentations thus created allow different colours to be used to separate sections of the text. The effect achieved is one which signals a complete break with the traditional way of producing text and illustration.

The poem describes a trans-Siberian journey during the Russo-Japanese war of 1904-05, ending with an evocation of the Eiffel Tower. At the top right-hand section of the work a map of the trans-Siberian railway is depicted, beginning in Moscow, winding through Siberia, to end at the Japanese sea. The painting climaxes in an image of the Eiffel Tower at the bottom left. The symbolism of the tower, erected in 1889, is carried to the extent that it dictated the physical size of the book: if 150 copies of the book were put end to end they would match its height. In the event, only 62 copies were created.

BLAISE CENDRARS
(1887–1961) AND
SONIA DELAUNAY
(1885–1979)

La prose du Transsibérien et de la petite Jehanne de France. Paris: Éditions des hommes nouveaux 1913. 1 folded sheet, col. ill.
Pressmark: Safe Room

La Prose du Transsibérien
et de la Petite Jehanne de France

Couleurs simultanées de Mme DELAUNAY-TERK

TIRAGE DE LUXE No III
De 1 à 8 pour les exemplaires parchemin
De 9 à 36 pour les exemplaires japon
De 37 à 150 pour les exemplaires simili japon

ÉDITIONS DES
HOMMES NOUVEAUX
4, rue de Savoie, 4
PARIS
1913
Tous droits réservés

En ce temps-là j'étais en mon adolescence
J'avais à peine seize ans et je ne me souvenais déjà plus de mon enfance
J'étais à 16 000 lieues du lieu de ma naissance
J'étais à Moscou, dans la ville de mille et trois clochers et des sep
Et je n'avais pas assez des sept gares et des mille et trois tours
Car mon adolescence était alors si ardente et si folle
Que mon cœur, tour à tour, brûlait comme le temple d'Éphèse ou comme la Place Rouge de Moscou
Quand le soleil se couche.
Et mes yeux éclairaient des voies anc
Et j'étais déjà si mauvais poète
Que je ne savais pas aller jusqu'au bout.

Le Kremlin était comme un immense gâteau tartare
Croustillé d'or
Avec les grandes amandes des cathédrales toutes blanches
Et l'or mielleux des cloches...
Un vieux moine me lisait la légende de Novgorode
J'avais soif
Et je déchiffrais des caractères cunéiformes

Puis, tout à coup, les pigeons du Saint-Esprit s'envolaient sur la
Et mes mains s'envolaient aussi, avec des bruissements d'albatros
Et ceci, c'était les dernières réminiscences du dernier jour
Du tout dernier vo
Et de la mer.

Pourtant, j'étais fort mauvais poète.
Je ne savais pas aller jusqu'au bout.
J'avais faim
Et tous les jours et toutes les femmes dans les cafés et tous les verres
J'aurais voulu les boire et les casser
Et toutes les vitrines et toutes les rues
Et toutes les maisons et toutes les vies
Et toutes les roues des fiacres qui tournaient en tourbillons sur les mauvais pavés
J'aurais voulu les plonger dans une fournaise de glaives
Et j'aurais voulu broyer tous les os
Et arracher toutes les langues
Et liquéfier tous ces grands corps étranges et nus sous les vêtements qui m'affolent...
Je pressentais la venue du grand Christ rouge de la révolution russe...
Et le soleil était une vilaine plaie
Qui s'ouvrait comme un brasier.

En ce temps-là j'étais en mon adolescence
J'avais à peine seize ans et je ne me souvenais déjà plus de ma naissance
J'étais à Moscou, où je voulais me nourrir de flammes
Et je n'avais pas assez des tours et des gares que constellaient mes yeux
En Sibérie tonnait le canon c'était la guerre
La faim le froid la peste le choléra
Et les eaux limoneuses de l'Amour charriaient des millions de charognes

Dans toutes les gares je voyais partir tous les derniers trains
Personne ne pouvait plus partir car on ne délivrait plus de billets
Et les soldats qui s'en allaient auraient bien voulu rester...
Un vieux moine me chantait la légende de Novgorode.

Moi, le mauvais poète qui ne voulait aller nulle part, je pouvais aller partout
Et aussi les marchands avaient encore assez d'argent
Pour aller tenter faire fortune.
Leur train partait tous les vendredis matin.
On disait qu'il y avait beaucoup de morts.
L'un emportait cent caisses de réveils et de coucous de la Forêt-Noire
Un autre, des boîtes à chapeaux des cylindres et un assortiment de tire-bouchons de Sheffield
Un autre, des cercueils de Malmoë remplis de boîtes de conserve et de sardines à l'huile.
Puis il y avait beaucoup de femmes
Des femmes des entre-jambes à louer qui pouvaient aussi servir
Des cercueils
Elles étaient toutes patentées
On disait qu'il y avait beaucoup de morts là-bas
Elles voyageaient à prix réduits
Et avaient toutes un compte-courant à la banque.

OR, UN VENDREDI MATIN CE FUT AUSSI MON TOUR
ON ÉTAIT EN DÉCEMBRE
ET JE PARTIS MOI AUSSI POUR ACCOMPAGNER LE VOYAGEUR EN BIJOUTERIE QUI SE RENDAIT À KHAR
NOUS AVIONS DEUX COUPÉS DANS L'EXPRESS ET 34 COFFRES DE JOAILLERIE DE PFORZHEIM
DE LA CAMELOTTE ALLEMANDE « MADE IN GERMANY »

IL M'AVAIT HABILLÉ DE NEUF ET EN MONTANT DANS LE TRAIN J'AVAIS PERDU UN BOUTON
— JE M'EN SOUVIENS, JE M'EN SOUVIENS, J'Y AI SOUVENT PENSÉ DEPUIS —
JE COUCHAIS SUR LES COFFRES ET J'ÉTAIS TOUT HEUREUX DE POUVOIR JOUER AVEC LE BROWNING NICKE
QU'IL M'AVAIT AUSSI DONNÉ

J'étais très heureux insouciant

Je croyais jouer aux brigands

Nous avions volé le trésor de Golconde

Et nous allions grâce au transsibérien le cacher de l'autre côté du monde

Je devais le défendre contre les voleurs de l'Oural qui avaient attaqué les saltimbanques de Jules
Contre les khoungouzes, les boxers de la Ch
Et les enragés petits Mongols du Grand-L
Alibaba et les quarante voleurs
Et les fidèles du terrible Vieux de la mon
Et surtout, contre les plus modernes
Les rats d'hôtel
Et les spécialistes des express internation

Et pourtant, et pourtant
J'étais triste comme un enfant
Les rythmes du train
La « moëlle chemin-de-fer » des psychiatres américains
Le bruit des portes des voix des essieux grinçant sur les rails congelés
Le ferlin d'or de mon avenir
Mon browning le piano et les jurons des joueurs de cartes dans le compartiment d'à côté

L'épatante présence de Jeanne
L'homme aux lunettes bleues qui se promenait nerveusement dans le couloir et qui me regardait en passant
Froissis de femmes
Et le sifflement de la vapeur
Et le bruit éternel des roues en folie dans les ornières du ciel
Les vitres sont givrées
Pas de nature !
Et derrière, les plaines sibériennes le ciel bas et les grandes ombres des Taciturnes qui montent et qui desce
Je suis couché dans un plaid
Bariolé

A Poem Machine

LILIANE LIJN
(*b*.1939)

Sky never stops:
Poemkon.
Text by Leonard D.
Marshall. London:
[the artist] 1965.
1 cone.
Pressmark: X940266

The work consists of a flat-topped cork cone, approximately 41 cm high with the diameter at the base 24 cm. The cone is painted white, with a poem Letrasetted in blue horizontally around it. The poem, by Leonard D. Marshall, reads: *Sky never stops, inner space outer space, same distance*. The cone is mounted on a motorised turntable which revolves the cone clockwise at a rate of 50 revolutions per minute.

In a short essay the artist describes the poem machines as follows:

SEE SOUND
AS MOVING LINES OF LIGHT

The words we utter travel in sound waves vibrating through the air to our inner ear.

When we see the written word we forget these letters are symbols of vibrations.

WORDS = VIBRATIONS = ENERGY

When I put words on cylinders and cones and make Poem Machines, I want the word to be seen in movement splitting itself into a pure vibration until it become the energy of sound.

1964–65 Poem-Machine takes on shape, becomes Poemkon. Conic shape bends itself to the dematerialisation of the word. At the narrowest point of the cone the words may still be readable whereas at the base they become a vibration pattern. The word accelerated loses its identity and becomes a patter pregnant with energy. It is pregnant with the energy of its potential meaning should it once again become a word.

I make Poem Machines to transform words into energy patterns.
In the Poem Machines the words we use are sublimated and become pure energy.

DISSOLVE THE IMAGES CREATED
BY WORDS
SEE SOUND

One of Liliane Lijn's major preoccupations as an artist has been to 'dematerialise volume'. The Poem Machines she created between 1962 and 1968 are perhaps the clearest manifestation of this. Here the words dematerialise as the verbal sequence turns into a line as the cone revolves. When the rotation slows down, the lines once again become distinguished as words.

String Book

Words are not necessary to make a book a book. In *Book 91, String Book*, the artist does not use words or ink. He attaches a number of pieces of string to a page which he then weaves through punched holes on the subsequent pages, attaching them again after weaving them through some pages subsequent to a page, attaching new strings there and continuing the weaving through the holes. The number of holes varies from page to page, sometimes only a single hole through which eight strings are fed and are led to the next page where they disperse and disappear into eight separate holes. As one opens the book and turns a page the friction of the string against the punched hole creates a sound.

The artist describes the book on an accompanying sheet.

Book 91 is a sequence of certain feelings and psychological experiences which I am not capable of placing *in words*; that is why I made the *book*. But as far as physical sensations are concerned the book is not about sound, but light. I consider all my books as photographic.

This book deals with cast light and shadows. The light spots are caused by viewing the book with a single light source at a 45° angle to the left of the book, three feet distant. The opened book reveals punched holes with deep shadows. As each page is lifted, however, dark holes throw circular spots of light across the facing page and the close environment of the book. The focus of these spots varies according to the distance from the page to the surface upon which they are cast. Like my books containing photographic film transparencies, the composition of each page is compounded and altered by the addition of and the movement of the shadow forms across the page.

I am concerned with the book-as-object. I am equally concerned with the book-as-experience. Here, the physical is used as transition …. The sound, cast light and shadows and their focus and movement, are not part of the physical book. They are physical, but they only come into existence during the act of experiencing the book, that is, turning the page.

KEITH A. SMITH
(*b*.1938)

Book 91. Barrytown, NY: Space Heater Multiples 1982. [24] leaves. Pressmark: X901035

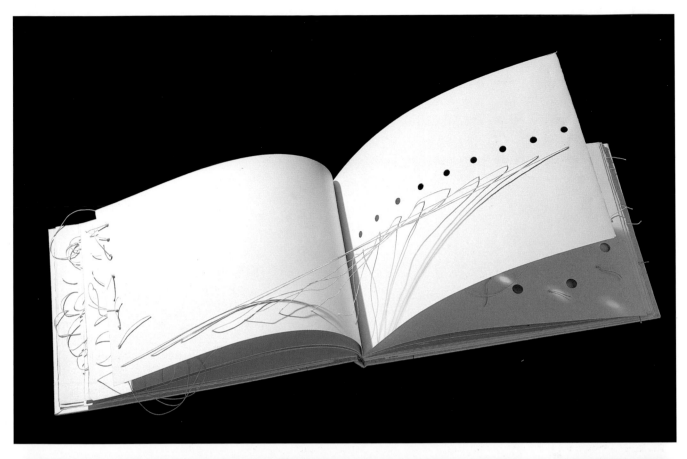

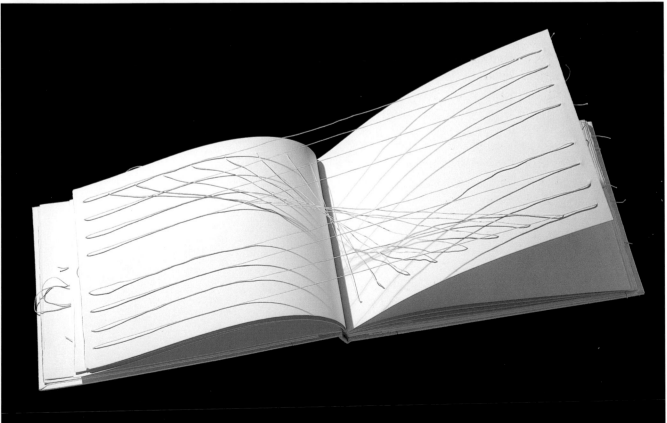

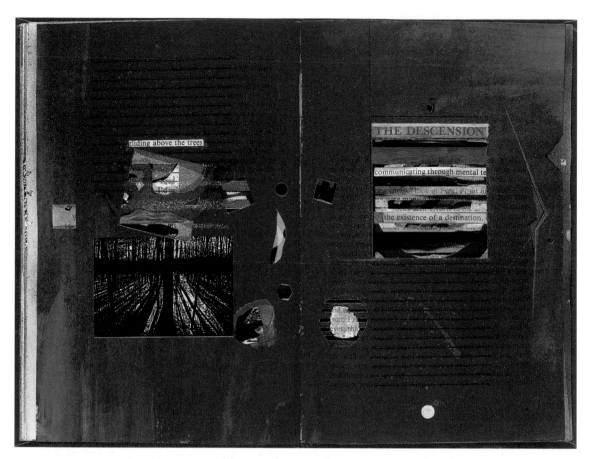

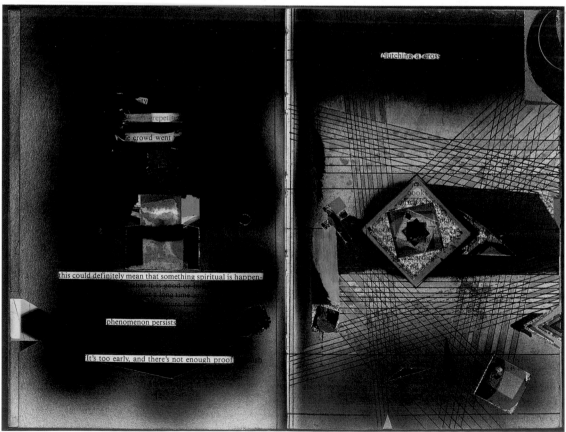

A Short Novel

JOHN ERIC
BROADDUS
(1943–1991)

*Above the Trees:
a Short Novel.*
[USA]: [the artist]
1985.
2 v., col. ill.
Pressmarks:
X891011-12

This is a unique sculpted book created by altering the structure of a conventionally published trade-edition book. The artist took a two-volume work, Edward J. Bohan's novel *The Descension* (1982), which he described as a 'horrid, vanity press novel about Armageddon', and airbrushed the text in such a way that a completely new work is created through the words and phrases of the original text which is allowed to remain.

The pages are richly embellished with images which are stuck on to the page, drawings, and sprayed-on pigment. The pages are also cut with a scalpel so that shapes appear in depth, three-dimensional squares, circles, triangles, oblong shapes and so forth. At once one can read the altered text on an extremely colourful page and see into the depths. Marvin Sackner, of The Sackner Archive of Concrete and Visual Poetry in Miami, relates in *The Altered Page*: 'With a bold palette, he paints the printed page… he also often dissects the page with a scalpel. He performs the intricate cuttings with the skill of a surgeon and does not remove the pages from the bound book. In response to my question as to how he deals with mistakes, his reply was that "I don't make mistakes". The artistry of his cuttings… is a testament to his assertion.'

An often-repeated image appearing throughout the work is a flying and floating figure which the artist describes as an 'endangered species' sign. 'I think of them as kind of in a limbo – floating and about to enter a new realm.' He was also inspired by Umberto Eco's acclaimed novel *The Name of the Rose* (1987), and uses floor plans based on the novel as an intrinsic part of the work.

Both volumes are housed in a protective slipcase which has been decorated with sequins and painted over in black. Both are finally protected in a painted cloth.

Mirror Book

The reader becomes the text! The work consists of 30 mirror-foil pages which are bound in glass mirror endboards riveted together. It is packed in a padded solander box and a pair of white gloves is provided for handling. As one turns the pages, hands are reflected, and on looking closely, our own faces. In the act of turning, the self-image becomes distorted. Here the book is the entrance key to a world of self-contemplation, and, potentially, self-knowledge.

The original prototype for this book was made for an exhibition held at the Victoria & Albert Museum in 1979, 'The Open and Closed Book'. It was then produced in a limited edition of 35 books in 1985.

JOHN CHRISTIE
(*b*.1945) AND RON
KING (*b*.1932)

Mirror Book/Book.
Guildford:
Circle Press 1985.
15 leaves.
Pressmark: X920105

Aunt Sallie's Lament

This book encapsulates in its format the contents of the text. Perhaps the hardest thing about an artist's book is to find the right language to describe it; and in this case it is practically impossible. The text is an autobiographical poem by a spinster quilter and the book's format resembles the diamond squares used in making a quilt. Each square, each a very clean colour, carries a muttering or observation by the quilter. As the page is turned one discovers that the pages are multishaped in order that the preceding statement can still be seen, thus providing new contexts with different associations. The binding is an accordion that allows the work to be stretched to 105 in., revealing all the stanzas. In her *catalogue raisonné* of the Janus Press (where this book was produced), Ruth Fine remarks that 'the structure controls the reading as the reading inspired the structure'.

The Janus Press, one of the most eminent, respected and innovative of the American private presses, was founded by Claire Van Vliet in 1955. Her work with illustrators, typographers, designers, binders, papermakers, and indeed writers, poets and novelists has been a hallmark of the Press since its founding. Because of this collaboration, the attention to detail and the resulting high quality of work is evident. One of the most striking collaborative ventures produced *Aunt Sallie's Lament*. The book was designed by Van Vliet based on a non-adhesive binding structure developed by Hedi Kyle and made with Linda Wray and Tamar Thorne. A special box was created by Judi Conant and Mary Richardson.

The critic Cathy Courtney describes the poem itself. 'It's an inner monologue spurred on by the sugary voice of a visiting dealer in search of Americana. Told by the phoney visitor that her artefacts are pretty and sweet, Aunt Sallie relives the key week of her life in which the dropping of her needle acted as pander to her happy seduction by "a potent medicine man". After his departure she "set aside that quilt, began another. / Never did I think it would unravel / Into a long on-looker's-life". Since no-one else matched up to the medicine man the rest of her days have been measured out in fragments of coloured fabric, the pace evoked by the methodical unwinding of the book.'

MARGARET
KAUFMAN

Aunt Sallie's Lament.
West Burke, Vermont:
Janus Press c.1988.
[23] p.
Pressmark: X890087

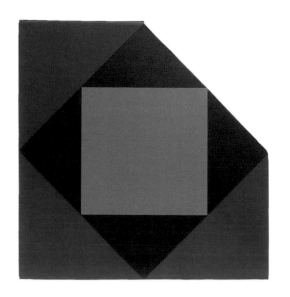

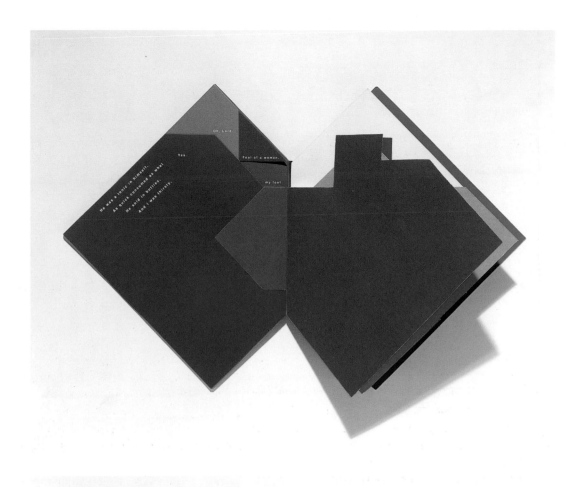

Killing

DENISE
HAWRYSIO (*b*.1957)

Killing III.
[London]: the artist
[1989?].
10 leaves.
Pressmark: X891017

The material from which a book is formed can create an inherent text and meaning. This is achieved with great success by the artist Denise Hawrysio in her series of four books entitled *Killing*. They form a wordless protest against our attitude to animal life and our ever-increasing massacring of creatures not only for food, but for *haute couture*, for the testing of fashion products or even simply for the sake of being able to display a trophy. No words are needed to convey the message to us: the work speaks for itself. In the work in the National Art Library the artist uses rabbit skin to make pages by gluing them back-to-back. Five such pages are bound together with a printed title on the cover: *Killing III*.

The other books in the series use leopard skin and Black Russian rabbit fur, while the fourth is made of imitation deer skin and is appropriately entitled *Imaginary Killing*.

Two Humument Globes

At the beginning of the 1960s, the artist Brion Gysin accidentally discovered the 'cut-up'. Printed words, from whatever source, could be cut up and removed from their context and put together to form a pool from which a writer could randomly withdraw words to be used collage-like in poems. In this way the poet was freed from the ramifications of conventional grammar. In 1960 William Burroughs, Gysin, Sinclair Beiles and Gregory Corso explored this technique in the publication *Minutes to Go*.

When Tom Phillips read an interview with Burroughs in the *Paris Review* (Fall 1965), which described this cut-up technique, he resolved to use it to make an artist's book. He set out to create a new work by artistically altering the pages of a Victorian novel, *A Human Document* by W.H. Mallock, published in 1892. Phillips called the altered work *A Humument* and published it in an edition of 100 in 1970.

The prospectus for the book describes it as follows: '*A Humument* is a treated work. A Victorian novel has been taken page by page and altered, adapted and metamorphosed; its text has been excavated for new ambiguities of character and situations and new ironies and paradoxes of utterance. In place of the unused part of Mallock's text an intricate web of visual iconography has sprung up, reminiscent of the varicoloured illuminations of Mediaeval and Oriental manuscripts.'

Phillips has continued to produce variants of *A Humument* over the years, reworking pages of Mallock's 1892 novel. *Two Humument Globes* are developments of these themes. The globes, made by Sylvia Sumira, are constructed from the pages of colour magazines which have been painted over, and texts and names from *A Humument* have been added to the surface creating imaginary universes. 'I found the names of strange countries and curious seas,' wrote Phillips, 'of fantasy islands and unvisitable cities as well as the features one should expect to find on a peopled planet.'

TOM PHILLIPS
(*b*.1937)

Two Humument Globes: Terrestrial and Celestial.
London: [the artist] 1992.
2 globes.
Pressmarks: X920275-76

Our Beautiful Homeland

ANDREW NORRIS
(b.1961)

Lijepa naša domovina
(Our Beautiful
Homeland).
1992–93.
[12] p., all ill.
Pressmark: X930043

This is a unique artist's book. The cover is made from plywood and canvas which have been covered with soil mixed with PVA and painted with acrylic. The book's 12 pages are photocopy paper which has also been covered with soil, with dried grass pressed on to them. They have been illustrated with found objects: fragments of wood, bricks and shattered glass, bread, corn straws, a bird's wings, a carnation, hair, gold chain, brambles. Barbed wire has been stitched to the page. The book is housed in a box, also treated with grass and soil, whose lid has terracotta tiles, bones, a necklace and a black-and-white photograph attached to it.

The artist has described the work as follows:

LIJEPA NAŠA DOMOVINA: Our Beautiful Homeland. The use of Croatia's National Anthem for the title of this book is incidental and is used ironically. It was inspired by a visit to Croatia in April 1992 and was created during that year while Bosnia was being systematically destroyed. I wanted to comment on the consequences when political regimes translate, through state-sponsored mythology, the individual's love of the homeland to that of a collective love of the country, and the manipulation of the population towards nationalism in its defence. My aim was to suggest something of the personal loss inflicted on all such individuals by focusing on a single detail, a personal possession, scattered on the grass, be it a gold chain or a button. Something we can all identify with to imply something much greater. With the huge displacement of people and destruction of homes, livelihoods and cultural monuments created by successive generations as a testament to multiculturalism, governments built new homogeneous states, replacing memory of the old with a new system of values, while individuals struggle to rebuild their lives. They have still not come to terms with their losses.

She's a Dish

*She is round
She is idealized
She hangs on the wall
She is not to be used
She is not disposable
She's a dish*

This work consists of six paper plates based on fourteenth- and fifteenth-century dishes known as *Belle Donne* or *Coppe Amatorie* depicting portraits of women. The poetic text (given above) surrounding the portraits on these paper plates resemble the painted scrolls on the original plates which indicated the woman's name followed or preceded by the adjective 'bella'.

In a descriptive sheet accompanying the paper plates, the artist explains: 'The invented text describes the plates, which were not realistic but idealized portraits or caricatures of the women. The portraits reflect the styles of dress influenced by court life in each area, and the styles of local artists. These plates were not destined for daily use – they were decorative dishes presented on special occasions such as courtship, engagement and marriage. They were not disposable like the paper plates of today, and neither were the images of women, as fashion changed so slowly during those centuries. It was common for the women to be portrayed as buxom, often with low-cut garments, simple jewellery and head coverings. The ceramicists copied the images from etchings available to them. These images started as prints, became ceramic plates, and return to print form once again, as paper plates.'

The book is presented in a narrow wooden crate suitable for shipping glass or china with slats on both sides through which the faces on the plates can be seen. The six plates are slotted into two sets of paper triptychs resembling wooden cupboards. The plates each have a handmade triangular brass hook which allows them to be displayed individually on a wall.

ANGELA LORENZ

*Paper Plates:
She's a Dish.*
Bologna: the artist
1993.
1 v.
Pressmark: X930215

9 Contemporary Art and Publishing

This chapter looks at the role publishing plays within the contemporary art world. Although not described as such at the time, one of the earliest books specifically about 'contemporary art' was Leon Battista Alberti's *De Pictura (On Painting)*, written in Latin in 1435. Since these humanist beginnings the relationship between the production of art and the production of books has remained close. Today the range of publications associated with contemporary art is vast, from practical techniques manuals through to sumptuous coffee-table picture books. The National Art Library has collected publications on contemporary art since its foundation in the mid-nineteenth century. Of course, at each historical moment what is regarded as 'contemporary' soon becomes dated. With this in mind, rather than attempt to provide a representative survey of all the many types of art publishing currently collected by the National Art Library, this chapter instead focuses on one particular art movement, the Young British Artists of the 1990s.

Much of the story of the Young British Artists' rise to fame can be told through their publications. The Movement emerged at a time when the gap between art and the other creative industries (music, fashion, design and architecture) was closing. In order to compete with these sectors for the public's attention, contemporary art became increasingly sensationalist and accessible. It was a time when Britain was rebranded 'Cool Britannia', and its artists received unprecedented coverage in the international media. London was perceived not just as a global financial centre, but also as a vibrant cultural melting pot. The increased popularity of contemporary art had a positive knock-on effect in the world of publishing. According to the Policy Studies Institute's *Cultural Trends* (no. 29, 1998), art showed the second-highest growth in sales (behind geography and atlases) with a 117 per cent increase over the period 1993–97. An astounding 3,507 art-related titles were published in the United Kingdom in 1997.

In the light of such figures, to select just ten items for this chapter was a difficult and necessarily exclusive task. Not only are large sectors of the art world not associated with the Young British Artists missing, but also whole areas of art publishing. Some of the best-selling art books are those relating to areas not covered in this essay, in particular, those relating to contemporary crafts, design and architecture. Also excluded are those many practical techniques manuals aimed at the art enthusiast, and popular picture books providing accessible introductions to art-historical themes and famous artists. However, through concentrating on the publications of the Young British Artists we can demonstrate how the art world uses the print medium both as a means of disseminating information and for creating publicity. Therefore, despite its limited focus, this chapter does examine the most important genres of art publishing today, including exhibition catalogues, artists' monographs, art journals, manifestos, pamphlets, museum catalogues, *catalogues raisonnés,* and art-historical surveys.

For artists – and just as significantly, their

dealers and collectors – publishing is chiefly important as a matter of record. Publications, although often overlooked, constitute the key means by which artists and art movements enter the canon of art history, thus ensuring that their works and ideas are represented in educational institutions such as art schools and museums. Who gets published and written about, and by whom, ultimately reveals the hierarchical nature of the art world. For artists to attract long-term critical attention through articles, reviews and catalogue essays, they need the support of critics and editors and the financial backing and support systems of gallery owners and publishers. Contemporary art books, because of the many illustrations they contain, the high production values required to reproduce art works at their best, and the often limited size of the audience they might appeal to (print runs rarely rise above 3,000 copies), are often subsidised by sponsors or public bodies like the Arts Council of England. When subsidy is not available, books on contemporary art can become very expensive. Even a popular success like Damien Hirst's *I want to spend the rest of my life* (see p.202) has a recommended retail price of £75.

For many artists who do not have access to either public subsidy or commercial backing, the only alternative is to 'do-it-yourself': to finance, produce, publish and distribute your own publications. The National Art Library also collects material in this area, most notably the series of artists' books produced by Matthew Higgs under the title *Imprint 93*, made in co-operation with many Young British Artists. As part of this series the Library

acquired in 1994 Martin Creed's notorious *Work no. 88,* a piece of A4 paper crumpled into a ball. The unconventionality of such works and their often problematic place within the Library indicates the contentious nature of contemporary art and its associated publications.

Because of their often short print runs, books on contemporary art can quickly go out of print and become unavailable. To collect in this area therefore requires a proactive approach informed by a knowledge of the latest exhibitions and the most promising up-and-coming artists. The best way to gain this knowledge is to visit exhibitions, talk to artists, curators and dealers, and read the contemporary art magazines. One particularly elusive genre is the exhibition catalogues of small galleries that rarely find commercial distribution. To collect in this area the National Art Library initiated an Exhibitions Catalogue Programme which identified and contacted art galleries around Britain requesting information about their publications. Many galleries now regularly send the Library their latest catalogues and private-view cards.

The relationship between art and publishing is synergetic, each benefiting from the energy and creativity provided by the other. However, whereas much of contemporary art is unique and of an ephemeral and site-specific nature, the book form will continue to provide a means of access and understanding that will survive beyond the specificity of a particular exhibition. For the foreseeable future at least, as long as art is made there will be books published to promote and explain its meanings.

Warehouse Shows

The inaugural exhibition of the Young British Art Movement was organised by a group of art students from Goldsmiths' College led by Damien Hirst. They called the exhibition 'Freeze' (parts 1 to 3 taking place between 6 August and 29 September 1988), and it was held in a soon-to-be-redeveloped Port of London Authority building in south-east London. The exhibition was partly funded by the Docklands Development Corporation. 'Freeze' was both a critical and financial success, and this type of warehouse show soon became established as a means of displaying contemporary art. Developers with property awaiting redevelopment were all too keen for artists to renovate and bring attention to their sites for exhibitions.

After 'Freeze', Hirst went into partnership with Carl Freedman, an old friend from Leeds, and Freedman's partner at the time, Billee Sellman, forming the company Sellman, Hirst and Freedman. Remembering this time, Freedman wrote: 'The company was a short-lived, critical and financial success, [f]ollowed by a rapid, out of control dive into bankruptcy. It was heady stuff, with a large warehouse gallery, vast overheads, grand openings and collectors arriving before shows had been barely installed and competing amongst each other to buy works.'

The company survived just three ventures between March and November 1990: namely the exhibitions 'Modern Medicine', 'Gambler' and 'Market' at Building One in Drummond Road, Bermondsey. It was at 'Gambler' that Charles Saatchi bought Hirst's now infamous dead-fly piece, *A Thousand Years*.

For each of these exhibitions a catalogue was produced. Artists and curators are well-versed in art history and realise that if an exhibition is to have a lasting significance beyond its often limited life-span, the temporality of the original display has to be transmuted into a permanent format. In this way it can reach many people and its contents travel further round the globe. In addition to documenting the contents of an exhibition, the catalogue can also provide a context and guide as to how the work should be interpreted.

MODERN MEDICINE

Curated by Billee Sellman, Damien Hirst and Carl Freedman.
London: [Sellman, Hirst and Freedman] 1990.
[40] p., chiefly ill.
Pressmark:
804. AA. 56

MODERN MEDICINE

Technique anglaise

Technique anglaise was the first book-length attempt to identify and document the new-found confidence amongst the Young British Artists in the wake of its growing international reputation. According to the co-editor, Andrew Renton, the rather cryptic title 'alludes to the French phrase for certain kinds of sexual games. The French perceive English technique as a repressive public school activity.'

The book consists of the transcript of a discussion between six artists, critics and gallery owners, Andrew Renton, Liam Gillick, Maureen Paley, Karsten Schubert, Lynne Cooke and William Furlong. This is supplemented with page works by 26 artists, where each artist was given six pages to represent their work in whatever way they saw fit. The artists selected were drawn from a small network associated with Goldsmiths' College and exhibitors in the exhibitions 'Freeze', 'Modern Medicine', 'East CountyYard' and other so-called 'warehouse shows'.

Co-published by one of the UK's foremost art-book publishers, Thames & Hudson, *Technique anglaise* played an important part in giving credibility to the developing Young British Artist Movement. With its selection of artists it also helped categorise a potentially heterogeneous body of work into some kind of recognisable style with a shared sensibility. Renton believed that a 'certain kind of irresponsibility seems to me to be a very key concept that brings all these people together, aesthetically. They're dealing with, if you like, irresponsible images, they're dealing with irresponsible constructions.'

As with many art movements, the artists themselves were very much involved with their historification. It is therefore significant that the book's co-editor (and designer) was the artist Liam Gillick. The transcript and interview genre predicted much of the journalistic style of commentary on the Young British Artists. Although now recognised as an informative and seminal Young British Artist document, it was not always thought of as such. In his review for *City Limits* (6-13 June 1991), Matthew Collings, later author of *Blimey!* (see p.201), described the book as 'fatuous and empty'.

ANDREW RENTON AND LIAM GILLICK, eds.

Technique anglaise: Current Trends in British Art.
London: Thames & Hudson 1991.
222 p., ill.
ISBN 0500973962.
Pressmark: NB.91.0573

TECHNIQUE ANGLAISE
CURRENT TRENDS IN BRITISH ART

EDITED BY
ANDREW RENTON & LIAM GILLICK

Frieze

Frieze was launched in the summer of 1991 with a pilot edition featuring on its cover a Damien Hirst 'butterfly' painting (from his 1991 exhibition 'In and Out of Love'). According to its website, *Frieze* is concerned with 'the cutting edge of current visual arts and its crossover with design, fashion, film, music and horticulture'. The founding editors were Matthew Slotover and Tom Gidley, both former students of St Martin's School of Art. In its initial phase, the magazine was closely associated with the rise of the Young British Artists (as is apparent from the obvious reference in its title to the exhibition 'Freeze').

Periodicals have always been very important for the promotion of an art movement, especially in its formative stages. The wider function of a contemporary art magazine is to record and comment on current events, promote certain artists and styles and generally lead and form public opinion. In this way an audience is built that identifies with the ideals and values of the magazine. The aim is to become an essential purchase, clearly differentiated from other magazines – in this case magazines such as *Art Monthly*, *Everything*, and *Modern Painters*.

With the eventual decline in interest in the Young British Artists, *Frieze* realised that the future was global, and concentrated on providing international coverage of the art world. The editors also realised that art was now just one element in a wider consumer market, and to reflect this they started running articles on a variety of lifestyle issues and subjects including advertising campaigns, training shoes and computer games. Art magazines also realised that they needed to compete with the style magazines if they were to keep their young audience's attention. A key element of *Frieze's* success is its use of smart graphic design and full colour illustrations throughout, both making it attractive to advertisers (just under 50 per cent of the magazine is now taken up with advertisements). Although the main advertisers remain art galleries, more recently the magazine has been attracting advertising from the likes of Sony, Prada and Helmut Lang.

FRIEZE: INTERNATIONAL ART MAGAZINE

London: Durian Publications 1991–present. v., ill. ISSN 0962-0672. Pressmark: PP.108.D

frieze

UK £3   US $6   AUS $10.95   NZ $12.95

ISSUE 1

VONG PHAOPHANIT   RICHARD PRINCE   THE TURNER PRIZE   WINDFALL

Charles Saatchi and the Young British Artists

The most influential collector of Young British Art is the advertising executive Charles Saatchi. Saatchi started collecting this type of work in the recession years of the early 1990s, when art by relatively unknown London artists could be bought cheaply and in bulk. Up to this date he was known mostly for his collection of contemporary work by established and thus expensive American and European artists. Saatchi's private gallery, a converted paint factory in north London, first opened in 1985. His intention was to promote and exhibit artists and work from his private collection.

This particular catalogue accompanied the first of what would turn into a series of six Young British Artist shows. The catalogue is very plain and would only have been available from the gallery during the exhibition. It is designed to be read while walking around and looking at the work. Its relative unpretentiousness can be contrasted with the sumptuous and expensive catalogue of his collection, *Young British Art: the Saatchi Decade,* published in 1999.

The rise to fame of these artists and the increasing value of their work is remarkable. It took just five years for them to go from being relative unknowns to media celebrities and establishment figures. Two of the artists in the show, Rachel Whiteread and Damien Hirst, went on to win the Turner Prize in 1994 and 1995 respectively. Saatchi's collection of Young British Art was celebrated in the controversial exhibition 'Sensation', held at the Royal Academy of Arts, London, in 1997.

This particular show is best remembered for its premiering of Hirst's *The Physical Impossibility of Death in the Mind of Someone Living* (1992), a 14-ft tiger shark preserved in formaldehyde. More than anything, Saatchi's collecting and exhibiting defined the Movement's parameters, making the Young British Artists the first art movement to be formed by a collector rather than by artists or critics.

SARAH KENT

Young British Artists: John Greenwood, Damien Hirst, Alex Landrum, Langlands & Bell, Rachel Whiteread. London: Saatchi Collection 1992. [16] p., ill. Pressmark: NL.92.0867

The Brit Pack

PATRICIA
BICKERS

The Brit Pack:
Contemporary British
Art, the View from
Abroad.
Manchester:
Cornerhouse 1995.
24 p., ill.
(Cornerhouse
communiqué ; no. 7).
ISBN 1897586221

The seemingly unstoppable rise of the Young British Artists did not occur without some concern being voiced in critical circles. Not everybody, it seemed, was seduced by these artists' quick transition from avant-garde rebels to establishment figures. The Young British Artists, as is apparent from their title, were primarily promoted as a national art movement. This is why the British Council, a publicly funded organisation set up specifically to promote British culture, was so forthcoming in funding exhibitions and travel abroad. The artists were used as cultural ambassadors to represent, and most importantly redefine, 'British' culture to an international audience (see exhibitions such as 'General Release', part of the 1995 Venice Biennale).

In *The Brit Pack*, Patricia Bickers, editor of *Art Monthly*, looked at the Movement through the eyes of foreign commentators, in order to contextualise the Young British Artist phenomenon and identify the key features of its formation. Bickers opens her essay with a complaint about a 'conspiracy of silence' in such magazines as *Art in America* over the British contribution to the Venice Biennale. She wondered if the critical silence surrounding the British involvement in the Biennale represented the start of a 'backlash' against the Young British Artists. Bickers wrote: 'How much longer can artists, most of them now in their thirties, be supposed to conform to this essentially adolescent role?' Given the polemical content of the essay it is fitting that it was issued as a pamphlet, the traditional means by which dissenting ideas are distributed. It is also, significantly, one of only three publications in this chapter to be published outside London.

It is interesting to note that the name of the Movement was still fluid at this point. Whereas Bickers preferred 'Brit Pack', others favoured 'neo-conceptual bratpack' (Sarah Greenberg), 'Britart' (Gordon Burn) and 'Britpop artists' (Waldemar Januszczak). It was not until after 1996 that the general consensus came to favour 'Young British Artists', or its more playful cousin 'yBa', as a label for the group.

THE BRIT PACK:

Contemporary British Art,
the view from abroad

Patricia Bickers

Cornerhouse, Manchester
Ffotogallery, Cardiff
Firstsite, the Minories, Colchester
John Hansard Gallery, University of Southampton
Manchester City Art Galleries
Oriel, the Arts Council of Wales' Gallery, Cardiff
Ormeau Baths Gallery, Belfast
Serpentine Gallery, London

Brilliant!

BRILLIANT!:
NEW ART FROM
LONDON

Minneapolis, Minn.:
Walker Art Center
1995. 91 p., ill.
Pressmark:
NM.95.0035

This catalogue was produced for a travelling exhibition that opened at the Walker Art Center, Minneapolis, in October 1995 and closed at the Contemporary Arts Museum, Houston, in January 1996. 'Brilliant' was an important exhibition that helped establish the Young British Artists in a potentially huge and lucrative market, the USA. Many commentators made connections with an earlier exhibition, 'London: The New Scene', that also took place at the Walker in 1965, and that celebrated the vitality of the London art world in the early 1960s.

Like that exhibition, 'Brilliant' happened at a time of great international interest in British art. According to the Walker's press release: 'Twenty-two young British invaders are set to storm the Walker Art Centre when "Brilliant! New Art from London" premieres. Witness work by a new generation of artists from the land that brought you Sid and Nancy, Chuck and Di, fish and chips, Hugh Grant and Cats. Gritty, funny, and in-your-face.' The catalogue essays by Stuart Morgan, Neville Wakefield and curator Richard Flood all sought to highlight the supposedly oppositional stance taken by the artists in relation to the gallery system.

To reinforce this marketing of the group as anti-establishment, the catalogue was designed and produced in a peculiar format, somewhere between a newspaper and a punk fanzine. Each artist was represented in the catalogue by a portrait photograph, an interview, and a selection of images of their choice. The transcript/interview format was preferred because of its spontaneity, authenticity and its clear link with celebrity culture. As Andy Warhol recognised, the interview does not always communicate information, but it does imply the importance of the interviewee. Interviews are also, lest we forget, easy to read and easy to write; they are the easiest way to produce copy. The cover of the catalogue caused some controversy as it juxtaposes the title of the exhibition with a photograph (supplied by artist Matt Collishaw) of the Baltic Exchange in the City of London wrecked by an IRA bomb in April 1992.

Spit Fire

A key feature of the London art world of the last ten years has been its promotion as a glamorous and 'happening' scene. Not since the 'swinging sixties', when artists such as David Hockney and Bridget Riley were regularly featured in colour supplements and magazines, has the work and lifestyle of contemporary artists attracted so much media attention. Evocative portrait photography has played a key role in the promotion of certain artists, in particular Damien Hirst and Sarah Lucas. In *Spit Fire*, Shand Kydd has attempted something similar to Lord Snowdon's documentation of the London art world of the 1960s in his book *Private View* (1965).

With grainy black-and-white photographs taken over a period of 17 months between March 1996 and July 1997, Shand Kydd presents a personal and fragmented portrait of a small and particular network of artists, critics and curators as they party their way through the London and international art world. Designed by Peter B. Willberg, the book and the photographs – like the informal fashion spreads they bear stylistic similarities to (called variously the 'grunge' or 'heroin chic' look) – carry minimal caption text. The photographer provides no introductory text and offers no explanation as to the significance of the personalities portrayed. Included amongst the many marginal and unknown figures associated with the scene are portraits of most of the 'art stars', including Tracey Emin, Gary Hume and Chris Ofili, the 1998 Turner Prize winner.

While appearing to catch the scene with its guard down – drinking at openings, chatting in studios and eating out in expensive restaurants – the book does little to reveal the importance of these social events for the art-world system. Events such as charity auctions, exhibition openings, talk programmes, and award dinners act as a breeding ground where artists can network with each other and with important art-world figures such as curators, dealers and collectors.

JOHNNIE SHAND KYDD

Spit Fire: Photographs from the Art World, London, 1996/97.
London: Thames and Hudson in association with Violette Editions 1997.
204 p., chiefly ill.
ISBN 050027990X.
Pressmark:
502.N.285.N

Spit Fire

Johnnie Shand Kydd

Photographs from the Art World London 1996/97

From Bohemia to Britpop:
The London Artworld from
Francis Bacon to Damien Hirst

BLIMEY!

Blimey!

MATTHEW
COLLINGS (b.1955)

Blimey!: From Bohemia
to Britpop, the London
Artworld from Francis
Bacon to Damien Hirst.
Cambridge: 21 Pub.,
Ltd 1997.
211p., col. ill.
ISBN 1901785009.
Pressmark: 502.B.189

Written in an anecdotal and conversational style, *Blimey!* sets out to be an accessible insider's guide to the movers and shakers of the London art world of the 1990s. In keeping with the majority of media attention on the Young British Artist scene, Collings concentrates on personalities rather than artworks. A substantial part of the book's appeal lies in Ian MacMillan's many colour photographic portraits of artists and art-world figures taken especially for the book. Again it is the lifestyle of the artist that attracts attention: a lifestyle based on that well-known figure of artistic legend, the Bohemian (the common denominator linking Francis Bacon with Damien Hirst in the book's subtitle).

Collings is a regular contributor to *Modern Painters*, where he writes an often humorous gossip column. His distinctive characteristic is that he writes about the art world with the enthusiasm of a participant. Indeed he even studied on the famed Goldsmiths' College MA course from 1990 to 1992 (one of his trademark 'target' paintings can be seen in the background of his portrait on the book's front cover). But Collings's *faux-naïf* style hides a long career in the arts media establishment. From 1983 to 1987 he edited *Artscribe International,* and between 1988 and 1996 he was a presenter and producer for BBC2's *Late Show.* More recently he presented and wrote the Channel 4 television series *This is Modern Art*.

In its very style the book echoes many of the characteristics of the Young British Artists: it is self-confident, dismissive of high/low cultural distinctions, idiosyncratic and resolutely non-political.

The publishing company '21' is a co-venture set up by pop star David Bowie, Sir Timothy Sainsbury, gallery-owner Bernard Jacobson, and Karen Wright, editor of *Modern Painters. Blimey!* was the company's first publication and its successful format, designed by Herman Lelie, was replicated in Collings's follow-up book, this time on the American art world, entitled *This Hurts*.

Damien Hirst

Damien Hirst and his dealer Jay Jopling are the most famous and commercially successful players in the British art world. Hirst first achieved recognition while still an art student at Goldsmiths' College, when he helped organise the important 'Freeze' exhibition in 1988. He soon followed this with exhibitions at the Institute of Contemporary Art, London (1991) and the Saatchi Gallery (1992). His meteoric rise to fame culminated in his winning the Turner Prize in 1995. At the Tate Gallery award ceremony he announced to millions of television viewers: 'It's amazing what you can do with an E in A-level art, a twisted imagination and a chainsaw.'

Since winning the Turner Prize he has diversified into making films, including the video for Blur's 'Country House' single of 1995, and opening restaurants, including Pharmacy in London's Notting Hill. Fittingly, considering his high media profile, Hirst chose the journalist Gordon Burn (best known for his books on the serial killers Peter Sutcliffe and Fred West) to write the introductory essay for his book, rather than an art critic or historian. As well as colour reproductions of all of his work up to 1997, the book contains many portrait photographs and press cuttings recording Hirst's controversial career.

Hirst designed the book in collaboration with the cutting-edge graphic designer Jonathan Barnbrook (a graduate of the Royal College of Art and director of the font company Virus). It incorporates many unconventional special effects, such as cut-outs, pop-ups and stickers. In an interview for the webzine *DZ3*, Barnbrook stated: 'We thought quite seriously about the role of art books and what they'd been like previously... thinking how we could change the perception of art books [by] being unpredictable.' In 1999, in recognition of its many innovations and high production values, the book won The New York Directors Special Award and The Tokyo Type Directors Club Gold Prize.

DAMIEN HIRST
(*b*.1965)

I want to spend the rest of my life everywhere, with everyone, one to one, always, forever, now.
London:
Booth-Clibborn
Editions 1997.
334 p., ill.
ISBN 1873968442.
Pressmark: X980030

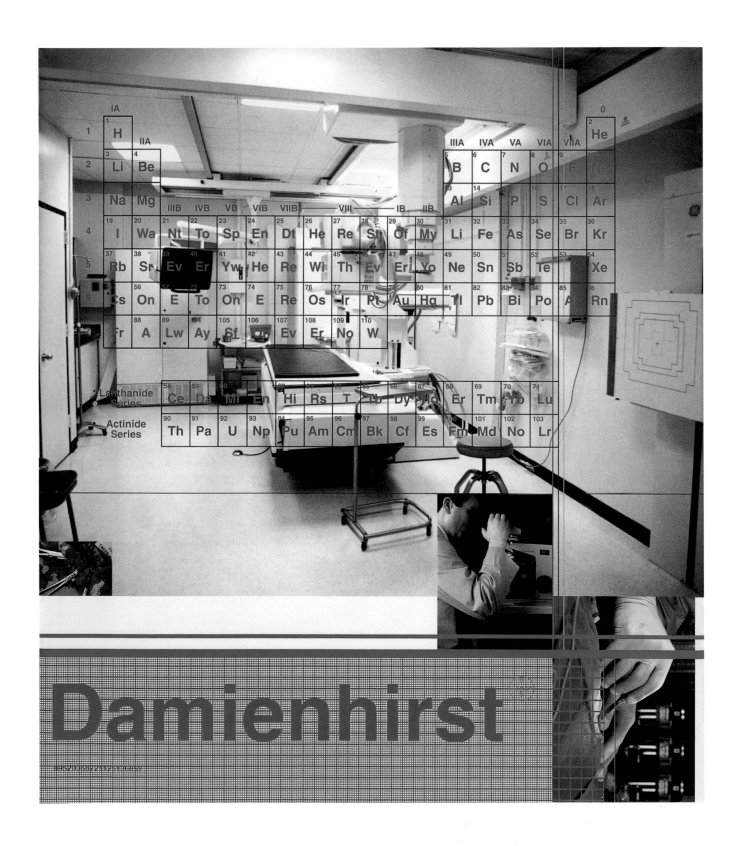

Popular Culture is for Idiots

One of the few artists' groups operating during the 1990s according to a historical avant-garde model was Bank, formed in 1992. With their chaotic group exhibitions, 'Wish You Were Here' (1994), 'The Charge of the Light Brigade' (1995) and 'Cocaine Orgasm' (1995), and their scurrilous news-sheet *Bank* which started in 1996, they have been a humorous irritant to the London art world.

This package, containing a press release and an invitation to a private view, is interesting on a number of levels. The text of the press release is written in the style of a manifesto. A manifesto can be defined as a public proclamation of an individual's or group's intentions and beliefs, and is designed to provoke and to stimulate the spectator. It has been a characteristic of twentieth-century avant-garde art movements to issue manifestos articulating their particular programmes, opinions and demands. This particular text sets out the group's ideas on collective practice, art and popular culture, and the recovery of the avant-gardist's project: 'It's not about the finished object. We don't see art as a unit of exchange. Art is how we live; it's our love affair with life. It is how we relate to life or the more interesting things in life and we believe in ART *[sic]*.'

The preview card shows the artists striking the threatening pose of a street gang in front of a gateway, the pillars of which are surmounted by carved skull and cross-bones. Constructing a strong image and identity is an important aspect of the contemporary artist's work. To get noticed by the media, artists

now have to be instantly recognisable. Often classed as ephemera and thought worthless, this type of material contains primary source information that will rarely be found in other sources. For many artists like Bank, who never quite make it to commercial success, this form of publicity can represent the only documentation of their practices that remains for future art historians to study.

FURTHER READING

Art Publishing & Art Publics Today (Transcript of a one-day conference held in the Lecture Theatre of the Victoria and Albert Museum on Saturday, 13 May 1989).

Barontini, Chiara. *The National Art Library and Its Buildings: from Somerset House to South Kensington* (London: NAL 1995).

Beatrix Potter, 1866–1943: the Artist and Her World (London: Frederick Warne with The National Trust 1987), ISBN 072323521X.

Blackwell, Lewis. *Twentieth-Century Type* (London: Laurence King 1992), ISBN 1856690261.

Bryant, Mark and Simon Heneage. *Dictionary of British Cartoonists and Caricaturists, 1730–1980* (Aldershot: Scolar Press 1994), ISBN 0859679764.

Bryant, Mark. *Dictionary of Twentieth-Century British Cartoonists and Caricaturists* (Aldershot: Ashgate 2000), ISBN 1840142863.

Burton, Anthony. *Vision & Accident: the Story of the Victoria and Albert Museum* (London: V&A 1999), ISBN 1851772928.

Cocks, Anna Somers. *The Victoria and Albert Museum, the Making of the Collection* (Leicester: Windward 1980), ISBN 0711200424.

Courtney, Cathy. 'The National Art Library', *Art Monthly*, no.125, April 1989, pp.31–32.

Darton, F.J. Harvey. *Children's Books in England: Five Centuries of Social Life* (3rd ed., rev. by Brian Alderson. London: British Library 1999), ISBN 0712346066.

Drucker, Johanna. *The Visible Word: Experimental Typography and Modern Art, 1909–1923* (Chicago, London: University of Chicago Press 1994), ISBN 0226165019.

Felmingham, Michael. *The Illustrated Gift Book, 1880–1930: with a checklist of 2500 titles* (Aldershot: Scolar Press 1988), ISBN 0704506270.

Ford, Simon and Davies, Anthony. 'Art Capital', *Art Monthly*, no.213, February 1998, pp. 1–4.

Gifford, Dennis. *The Complete Catalogue of British Comics Including Price Guide* (Exeter: Webb & Bower 1985), ISBN 086350079X.

Gifford, Dennis, *Encyclopedia of Comic Characters* (Harlow: Longman 1987), ISBN 058289245.

Goldman, Paul. *Victorian Illustrated Books 1850–1870: the Heyday of Wood-Engraving* (London: British Museum Press 1994), ISBN 0714126004.

Goldman, Paul. *Victorian Illustration: the Pre-Raphaelites, the Idyllic School and the High Victorians* (Aldershot: Scolar Press 1996), ISBN 0859678644.

Harthan, John P. *Bookbindings* (3rd ed. London: HMSO 1985), ISBN 011290226X.

Harthan, John P. *The History of the Illustrated Book: the Western Tradition* (London: Thames & Hudson 1981), ISBN 0500233160.

Harthan, John P. *An Introduction to Illuminated Manuscripts* (London: HMSO 1983), ISBN 0112903967.

Hobbs, Anne Stevenson and Joyce Irene Whalley. *Beatrix Potter: the V&A Collection. The Leslie Linder Bequest of Beatrix Potter Material* (London: V&A and Frederick Warne 1985), ISBN 0723232601.

Hobbs, Anne Stevenson, ed. *Fables* (London: V&A 1986), ISBN 094810712X.

Hodnett, Edward. *Five Centuries of English Book Illustration* (Aldershot: Scolar Press 1988), ISBN 0859676978.

Hogben, Carol and Rowan Watson, eds. *From Manet to Hockney: Modern Artists' Illustrated Books* (London: V&A 1985), ISBN 0948107081.

Horn, Maurice, ed. *The World Encyclopedia of Cartoons* (New York: Chelsea House 1980), ISBN 0877540888.

Horn, Maurice, ed. *The World Encyclopedia of Comics* (Philadelphia: Chelsea House 1998), ISBN 079104856X.

James, Elizabeth. *The Victoria and Albert Museum: a Bibliography and Exhibition Chronology, 1852–1996* (London: Fitzroy Dearborn in association with the V&A 1998), ISBN 1884964958.

Lomas, Elizabeth. *Guide to the Holdings of the Archive of Art and Design* (forthcoming).

Marks, P.J.M. *The British Library Guide to Bookbinding: History and Techniques* (London: British Library 1998), ISBN 0712345825.

National Art Library. *A Diversity of Gifts: Four Benefactors of the National Art Library …* (London: NAL 1995), ISBN 1851771638.

Physick, John. *The Victoria and Albert Museum, the History of its Building* (London: [V&A] 1982), ISBN 0905209257.

Sendak, Maurice. *Caldecott & Co.: Notes on Books and Pictures* (London: Reinhardt in association with Viking 1989), ISBN 1871061067.

Turner, Silvie, ed. *Facing the Page: British Artists' Books: a Survey 1983–1993* (London: estamp 1993), ISBN 1871831113.

Van der Wateren, Jan. 'Archival resources in the Victoria and Albert Museum.' *Art Libraries Journal*, vol.14, no.2, 1989, pp.16–27.

Van der Wateren, Jan and Rowan Watson, eds. *The National Art Library: a Policy for the Development of the Collections* (London: NAL 1993), ISBN 0952120909.

Victoria & Albert Museum. *Charles Dickens: an Exhibition to Commemorate the Centenary of his Death, June–September 1970* (London: HMSO 1970).

Victoria and Albert Museum. *The Open & Closed Book: Contemporary Book Arts* (London: HMSO 1979).

Watson, Rowan. *Vandals and Enthusiasts: Views of Illumination in the Nineteenth Century* (London: V&A 1995), ISBN 1851771670.

Wedgwood, Alexandra. *A.W.N. Pugin and the Pugin Family* (London: V&A 1985), ISBN 0948107014.

Whalley, Joyce Irene. *Catalogue of English Non-Illuminated Manuscripts in the National Art Library up to December 1973 [and supplements of accessions for 1974, 1975 and 1976]* (London: V&A 1975–1976).

Whalley, Joyce Irene and Vera Kaden. *The Decorated Page: Eight Hundred Years of Illuminated Manuscripts and Books* (London: V&A 1971).

Whalley, Joyce Irene and Tessa Chester. *A History of Children's Book Illustration* (London: John Murray with the V&A 1988), ISBN 0719545846.

Whalley, Joyce Irene and Vera Kaden. *The Universal Penman: a Survey of Western Calligraphy from the Roman Period to 1980* (London: HMSO 1980), ISBN 0112903398.

White, Eva. *From the School of Design to the Department of Practical Art: the First years of the National Art Library, 1837–1853* (London: NAL 1994).

Williams, Emmett, ed. *An Anthology of Concrete Poetry* (New York: Something Else Press 1967).